How The Other Half Loves

A Comedy

Alan Ayckbourn

Samuel French - London
New York - Toronto - Hollywood

ISBN 0 573 11166 9

Please see page iv for further copyright information.

HOW THE OTHER HALF LOVES

This play was presented by Peter Bridge at the Lyric Theatre, London, on 5th August, 1970, with the following cast:

Frank Foster	Robert Morley
Fiona Foster	Joan Tetzel
Bob Phillips	Donald Burton
Teresa Phillips	Heather Sears
William Featherstone	Brian Miller
Mary Featherstone	Elizabeth Ashton

Directed by Robin Midgley
Designed by Alan Tagg
Lighting by John B. Read

The action of this play takes place in the living-rooms of the Fosters and Phillips

ACT I   Scene 1 Early Thursday morning
           Scene 2 Evening

ACT II Scene 1 Saturday morning
           Scene 2 Sunday morning

Time—the present

ACT I

SCENE 1

The living-rooms of the Fosters and Phillips. It is early Thursday morning

The Lights come up on the main set to reveal two living-rooms. Not a composite setting but two rooms contained and overlapping in the same area. Only the furnishings themselves, both in colour and style, indicate which belongs to which room. The Fosters' furniture is smart period reproduction, while the Phillips' is more modern, trendy and badly looked after. Both rooms have similar items. DR *is the Phillips' dining-table and two chairs. To* L *of the Phillips' the table is a three-seater settee with the* R *two seats matching the Fosters' decor and the* L *seat matching the Phillips' decor.* C *is an armchair (Foster) and* L *is another armchair (Phillips).* R *of the* C *chair is a small table (Foster).* UL *is the Fosters' dining-table and two chairs.* DC *is a composite coffee-table with the Phillips' section* R *and the Fosters' section* L. *On each section is a phone.* DL *is the Phillips' child's playpen and toys including a doll's house and the Phillips' armchair. Each room has two doors and a window as follows:* DR *the Phillips' window,* R *the Fosters' kitchen door,* UR *the Phillips' front door,* UL *the Fosters' front double doors,* L *the Phillips' kitchen and* DL *the Fosters' window*

The Fosters' main door opens and Fiona, an elegant woman in her forties, enters in her dressing-gown. She goes to the window L *and draws the curtains. The Lights come up on the Fosters' areas. She crosses to the phone and dials. The phone in the Phillips' house starts to ring. After a second, Teresa, an untidy, rather intense, tired-looking woman in her early thirties, enters from the kitchen door* L *carrying a mug of tea. She is in a different room to Fiona and so does not acknowledge her presence in any way. The characters in their different rooms will often pass extremely close but without ever actually touching. Teresa picks up her receiver*

Teresa Hallo. Hallo . . .

Fiona hangs up with a sigh. She looks at her watch. Teresa, frowning, crosses to her curtains R *and draws them. The Lights come up on the Phillips' areas. She reacts to the bright early-morning light. She switches on her portable radio which is on the dining-table. It is a news programme*

> *Fiona, who has been standing thoughtfully, turns and goes out into the kitchen* R

Teresa sits reading a newspaper cutting and drinking tea

> *The Fosters' double doors fly open again and Frank enters like a whirlwind.*

He is dressed in running shorts, a vest and a jaunty sporting cap and is breathing heavily

As he enters, the kitchen timer which is on the coffee-table, rings. Frank reaches it and it stops ringing. He surveys it in digust and then switches on the radio on the coffee-table. Loud military music. He picks up a skipping rope from the coffee-table and with an effort, starts to skip

After a moment, Fiona re-enters. She takes in Frank with a frown, goes to the coffee-table and, almost unconsciously, switches the radio off

Fiona That's rather grotesque, darling. Do you have to do that first thing in the morning? I'm sure you'll damage yourself one of these days. It's twenty past. Did you know?

Frank That's rather why I switched the radio on. (*He sits on chair* C)

Fiona (*without pausing on her way out*) All right. So long as you know.

Fiona goes out into the hall UL

Teresa (*crossing to the bedroom door and calling*) Bob! Bob! It's twenty-five past—Bob! Get up!

She gives up after hearing no reply and goes out L

Fiona enters immediately with the newspapers which she tosses on to the settee

Fiona Frank, I'll have to have the car this morning.

Frank Oh yes?

Fiona I've got an awful lot of dashing around to do.

Frank Well, you—haven't got to dash around this morning, have you?

Fiona I have to dash around every morning, darling, but this is more frantic than usual.

Frank It's jolly inconvenient, as it happens . . .

Fiona Yes, it's jolly inconvenient for both of us, darling. But I just can't manage without it.

Frank (*picking up phone and starting to dial*) As long as that's perfectly clear. I mean you're not the only one that has to dash around, you know. I mean there are times when I'm—dashing around . . .

Fiona Yes, well, I'll get us some breakfast. You ought to get dressed.

She goes out into the kitchen R

The Phillips' phone rings

Frank (*muttering*) Quite frequently—dashing around . . .

Bob, in his early thirties, enters blearily from the kitchen L. *He switches off Teresa's radio*

Bob (*answering the phone*) Hallo.

Frank (*startled*) Hallo. Who's this?

Bob What?

Frank Who am I talking to?

Bob Good-morning, Frank. This is Bob Phillips.

Frank Ah, good-morning, Bob. I'm glad you rang, I wanted a word. I've asked everyone to get to the office a little earlier this morning. I tried to catch you yesterday. What happened to you? Sneak off a bit early, did you?

Bob Yes I had—to meet someone . . .

Frank Oh yes? I won't ask who. (*He laughs*)

Bob laughs

Listen Bob, can you be in by a quarter past?

Bob I'll try.

Frank I'd like the whole team there. Full strength. Right?

Bob Right. (*He goes to hang up*)

Frank Oh, Bob . . .

Bob Yes?

Frank Do you know anything about Featherstone?

Bob Do I know about what?

Frank Featherstone. Bright little chap from Accounts. Do you know him at all?

Bob Oh, William Featherstone. Yes.

Frank What's your opinion of him?

Bob (*surprised*) He's all right.

Frank Good man, is he?

Bob Fine—as far as I know.

Frank (*hanging up*) Good. Good. Good. (*He rises, switches on his radio, takes it with him, and goes towards the hall, muttering*) I'm frequently dashing around.

He goes out to the hall UL

Bob is left holding the receiver for a moment

Teresa enters from L *engrossed in the paper, her mug of tea still in her hand*

Bob (*replacing the receiver*) Morning.

Teresa (*without looking up*) Hallo. (*She sits on* L *end of the sofa*) Who was that?

Bob Just business.

Teresa Oh.

Bob Any tea?

Teresa Just made it.

Bob Oh. Good.

Teresa On the stove. My God, there's another letter from this woman. That's about three this week already.

Bob On the stove?

Teresa What?

Bob The tea?

Teresa That's right. Help yourself.

Bob breaks L *and turns back*

Oh no, honestly, that's incredible. She's raised six hundred pounds just in coffee mornings amongst her friends. Isn't that incredible?

Bob (*crossing to* L *of Teresa*) Perhaps you ought to do the same thing with tea mornings? Invite me along. That way I might even get a cup.
Teresa It's on the stove.
Bob Fine. Fine.

Fiona enters from kitchen R *with a loaded tray and crosses* L. *Bob crosses* L *and goes into kitchen* L. *Fiona puts the tray on table* L *and begins to unload it*

Teresa (*engrossed again in her newspaper*) Oh—no! Honestly . . .

Frank comes in through the main door

Frank (*crossing towards the kitchen* R) Darling—Darling?
Fiona Hallo?
Frank (*crossing to* R *of Fiona*) It would appear that I have no clean shirt. Is that in fact the case?
Fiona Hmm?
Frank No clean shirts. I have no clean shirts, apparently.
Fiona Well, darling, if you'd like to pop upstairs again and look on the third shelf down, I think you'll find no less than three shirts, all nice and clean and still wrapped up in cellophane bags from the laundry.
Frank Third shelf?
Fiona That's right.
Frank What the devil are they doing on the third shelf?
Fiona Presumably lying there, waiting for you to put them on, darling.
Frank What are they doing on the third shelf. What's wrong with the second shelf . . .?
Fiona Nothing at all as far as I know darling, but since nineteen fifty-seven your shirts have always been kept on the third shelf down. They have not been kept on the second shelf down since we moved from Woking.
Frank Woking?
Fiona (*crossing to kitchen door* R) We weren't so well off in Woking, if you remember. You had a smaller wardrobe . . .
Frank (*crossing to* UC) I don't know anything about Woking . . .

Fiona goes out R *with the empty tray*

Fiona (*as she goes*) You go and have a look.
Frank Why the hell does she have to drag Woking into the conversation.

Frank tramps out UL, *disgruntled*

Bob enters from kitchen L *and crosses slowly to* L *of Teresa*

Bob I see you're hanging on with grim nostalgia to that empty cornflake packet.
Teresa Mmmm? Oh, that. I didn't have time.
Bob Ah.
Teresa Did you get your tea?
Bob No. It appears you only made enough for one.
Teresa No, I didn't . . .

Bob That was the impression I got from the teapot, anyway. I did toy with the idea of chewing the leaves but decided to make some fresh instead. (*He crosses to the dresser* UR *for a cigarette*)

Fiona enters from the kitchen R *with a tray, and crosses to the table* L

Bob crosses to US *of Teresa who closes the newspaper*

Teresa Is Benjamin awake?
Bob Haven't heard him.
Teresa He's marvellous these days. It used to be four o'clock, didn't it?
Bob So I remember telling you at the time.
Teresa I got up now and again, as well . . .
Bob Now and again.
Fiona (*going out* R, *calling*) Frank—breakfast.

Bob goes to the dresser for matches

Fiona goes out to the kitchen R

Bob crosses to DR *of the sofa*

Teresa Did you want some breakfast, then? Is that what this is all about?
Bob Not if—you're rushed off your feet.
Teresa Well, there's no need to go on at me. I mean considering the fact that you rolled in here at two o'clock this morning stinking drunk and I haven't said a word about it . . .
Bob Till now . . .
Teresa Haven't said a word about it, I think it's really a bit of a nerve to sit there complaining there isn't any breakfast.
Bob I'm not complaining.
Teresa Good.

Bob crosses L *and pauses* L *of the* C *chair*

Fiona enters from the kitchen R *with egg and toast on a tray. She crosses to the table* L

Bob (*going out* L) What on earth have I to complain about?

Bob goes out L

Fiona Frank—it's on the table. (*She goes to the doors* UL)
Frank (*off*) Coming.

Fiona goes to the phone and dials. Teresa's phone rings. Teresa answers it

Teresa Hallo . . .

Fiona is about to replace the phone as:

Frank enters UL, *pulling on his jacket*

Fiona (*into the phone*) Eight twenty-eight and twenty seconds . . . (*She seems to adjust her watch*)
Teresa What? Hallo?

Fiona replaces the receiver

Hallo? (*After a second she replaces the receiver, puzzled, and then resumes her reading*)

Fiona (*crossing to the table* L) Eight twenty-eight and twenty seconds . . .

Frank (*crossing to the* C *chair and moving the small table from* R *to the front of the* C *chair*) Is that what it is?

Fiona Yes.

Frank Oh. Damn fool on the wireless has just said it's eight thirty-three. (*He sits in the armchair*)

Fiona picks up the tray and crosses to L *of Frank and puts the tray on his table, and then crosses back to the table* L, *sits and pours coffee*

Fiona Well, they can't both be right . . .

Frank Hardly. Ah! (*He tackles his egg*)

Fiona butters herself some toast, and pours coffee

Bob enters from the kitchen L *and crosses to* C, *waves his mug at Teresa and then crosses and sits in the armchair* DL

Bob Benjamin's awake now.

Teresa Is he crying?

Bob No just beating on the floor with his wet nappy.

Teresa Oh, well, I'll leave him for a minute. Get you your bloomin' breakfast.

Bob As I say. Don't go out of your way . . .

Teresa Oh, shut up. Some woman rang up just now.

Bob Woman.

Teresa Yes. Told me the time and rang off.

Bob Tim's mother, do you think?

Teresa Oh no, it wasn't that. Anyway, you're supposed to ring them, aren't you?

Bob It's customary. Was she abusive as well—lewd suggestions?

Teresa No. (*She rises and drops the newspaper* R *of Frank*) She was a couple of minutes fast . . .

Bob No-one I know.

Teresa I didn't imagine it would be.

Teresa goes out L

Fiona rises, gives some coffee to Frank and then crosses R *and sits the* R *end of the sofa with her coffee and reads a newspaper. Bob sips his tea. Frank sniffs at his egg*

Fiona It's perfectly fresh.

Frank Just make sure. Always make sure first.

Fiona Yes, I've noticed.

Frank Yes. This is fine. Good fresh egg this.

Fiona Good.

Frank (*eating*) Very nice. Very nice indeed.

Bob rises, crosses to C *and picks up the newspaper and then sits again* DL.
Fiona reads the paper

Pity you couldn't get home till late last night.

Fiona Oh? Why's that?

Frank Well, with being—er—well no point in it really. Sentimental. No, no, no . . .

Fiona Being what?

Frank Oh, I don't know why. Always seem to get a bit gooey over these sort of things. I don't know why. It's the women who're supposed to be gooey, aren't they?

Fiona Darling, gooey about what?

Frank Our wedding anniversary.

Fiona (*in a dead tone*) Oh, Lord.

Frank (*laughing, embarrassed*) Silly, isn't it?

Fiona Oh, Lord.

Frank No matter. I—er, bought some special plonk actually. You know, some of your—special plonk . . .

Fiona Did you?

Frank Matter of fact I—drank the lot. Rather merry. Opened it up—let the air in and so forth—comes eleven-thirty—not a drop. Thought, well, if she walks in now, sees I've drunk all her special plonk—me for the doghouse, eh?

Fiona I got held up, I'm afraid.

Frank Yes, I thought you'd been held up. Another meeting was it?

Fiona Umm . . .

Frank No. It couldn't have been a meeting, because your Mrs Thingamyjig rang up and said you weren't there and where were you, and I remember saying to her that I thought you must have been held up.

Fiona Mrs Who?

Frank Can't remember offhand. Mrs Thingamyjig . . .

Fiona Oh, Lord. (*She continues to read the paper rather angrily*)

Teresa enters from kitchen L *and crosses to* R *of Bob with sandwich on a plate*

Teresa I had to get Benjamin up. Put him in his chair. He's tearing the wallpaper up there. I think he's bored. We ought to find something to amuse him. Something on elastic he can twang. Amy Murchison gave her kid an old bra of hers and a couple of tennis balls. Kept it happy for hours. Bit Freudian, though, isn't it? Here you are. (*She holds the plate out to Bob*)

Bob What's that? (*He puts the newspaper on the floor*)

Teresa (*still holding out the plate*) Your breakfast. I made you a sandwich.

Bob What sort of sandwich?

Teresa Peanut butter.

Bob (*staring at it*) Peanut butter?

Teresa It's all we seem to have.

Bob You shouldn't have gone to all this trouble, you know.

Teresa (*dropping the plate and sandwich into Bob's lap almost casually*) Don't have the damn thing, then. (*She snatches up the paper and sits at the* L *end of the settee*)

Bob stares at the sandwich, thoughtfully. Frank has finished his egg with a flourish and turns his attention to the toast

Frank This toast all right?
Fiona Perfectly.
Frank Seems a bit dried out. Dry you know.
Fiona I should damp it down then, darling, if I were you.
Frank (*doubtfully*) Um.

Bob rises and crosses to the L *of Teresa with the plate*

Bob Never mind. It was a beautiful thought.
Teresa Don't you like peanut butter?
Bob Not round about now I don't.
Teresa That's funny. Benjamin adores it . . .
Bob Does he?
Teresa Yes. Out of a spoon. He can't get enough of it.
Bob Well, I obviously don't take after Benjamin. I'll put it next to the cornflake packet. As a memento. (*He crosses* L *and turns back*) I don't know what you're reading that for. You've read one newspaper, you've read the lot.

He exits into kitchen L

(*Off*) There's a report in there of this fellow's speech—exactly the same speech that was reported in yesterday's paper . . .
Teresa This is yesterday's paper.

Bob appears in the kitchen doorway L

Bob Yesterday's?
Teresa I hadn't finished reading it.
Bob Well, where the hell's today's?
Teresa I don't know. Outside, probably.
Bob Oh my God—

He goes out L

Teresa (*calling after him*) See Benjamin's all right, will you?

Fiona folds up the paper

Frank That toothbrush is on the blink by the way.
Fiona Um?
Frank I'll have to look at it after breakfast. Electric toothbrush. On the blink.
Fiona Oh, is it?
Frank Battery's flat by the sound of it. Hardly a flicker out of it.
Fiona No?
Frank No. Had to clean my teeth with the flannel.

Fiona Your own I hope.
Frank Oh yes. The blue one.
Fiona That's the bath cloth.
Frank Ah! Is it? Is it! (*He is thoughtful, sucking his teeth speculatively*)

Bob comes in from the kitchen L

Bob (*crossing to* US *of the table* L) Benjamin's poured his prunes all over his head.
Teresa (*leaping up*) Oh no—

Teresa drops the paper and goes out to the kitchen L

Bob (*following her*) Perhaps he prefers peanut butter . . .

Bob goes out into the kitchen L

Frank Where did you get to then?
Fiona When?
Frank Last night?
Fiona Oh, I got held up . . .
Frank Oh. (*He pauses*) I see. Doesn't matter.
Fiona It's no secret. There's no secret about it.
Frank Isn't there?
Fiona No. No secret at all. (*She rises and crosses to* R *of Frank putting her cup on the coffee-table*)
Frank Good.
Fiona More coffee? (*She picks up tray and crosses to* DS *of the table* L *and pours coffee*)
Frank Ah, thank you.

Bob enters laughing from the kitchen L *and crosses to* UR *of Frank. Teresa follows him and crosses to the table* DR

Teresa I don't know what you think is so damn funny.
Bob I think the prune juice suits him.
Teresa (*sourly*) Oh ha-ha. (*She grabs handful of tissues from the box on the table* DR *and crosses* L) You're no help. No help at all.

Teresa goes out L

Bob turns and goes out UR

Frank Oh that reminds me, I mustn't forget to give you your present.
Fiona Present?
Frank Your anniversary present. I must give you that before I go.
Fiona (*crossing to* L *of Frank with the coffee*) There's no need to rub it in, darling.
Frank What? Oh. That wasn't my intention. Wasn't my intention to rub it in.

Fiona collects her own cup from the coffee-table and crosses to the table L

Bob enters UR *with a new newspaper and crosses* DS *to the phone*

Fiona Good.
Frank Good Lord, no.

Teresa enters from kitchen L *and crosses to the wastepaper basket* DR

Bob drops the phone and opens the paper

Teresa Where the hell were you last night, anyway?
Bob Me?
Teresa Where were you?

Bob crosses and sits in the armchair DL. *Fiona crosses and sits at the* R *end of the sofa*

Bob What a funny question.
Teresa (*crossing to* L *of the sofa*) No, I'm sick of this. Other husbands tell
   their wives where they go to. They don't just disappear and come
   blundering in at two o'clock in the morning. Other husbands . . . (*She
   crosses to* R *of Bob and pulls her apron off the back of the armchair*) I
   mean here am I stuck here with Benjamin and you're out having parties
   and God knows what else and here am I stuck here.
Bob What's all this in aid of? (*He rises and crosses* DR *takes his jacket from
   the chair* DS *of the table and puts it on*)
Teresa He's your child as much as mine.
Bob I believe you.
Teresa (*crossing to* L *of* C) Well, where were you? I want to know. Where
   were you?
Bob (*indignantly*) Out.
Teresa Just out?
Bob (*crossing to* R *of Teresa*) That's right.
Teresa What doing?
Bob Drinking, talking . . .
Teresa Who with?
Bob Why do you want to know?
Teresa Because I'm not a fool you know. I'm not a complete fool. I mean
   I'd be very stupid indeed if I didn't notice——

A crash off

Oh no! Wait a minute.

She hurries off L

(*Off*) Benjamin! Benjamin, you stop that at once . . .

Bob meanders and sits at the L *end of sofa*

Frank (*rising and crossing* US) I think I will get it for you, though. All the
   same the present . . .

Frank goes out UL

Fiona rises and crosses to DS *of the table* L *and puts down her cup, dropping
the newspaper on the* C *chair on her way*

Fiona (*annoyed with herself*) Oh.

Teresa enters from the kitchen L *with a large spoon and crosses to* L *of Bob*

Fiona crosses and picks up the papers

Teresa I caught him trying to swallow this.

Bob Really?

Teresa He could have choked. Easily.

Bob I think he'd have stood a good chance.

Teresa You don't care. You don't care at all, do you? You don't care. You don't care about me, you don't care about Benjamin . . . (*She crosses to the armchair* DL *and throws the spoon in the playpen*) You just don't care. (*She sits* DL)

Pause. Fiona sits in the C *chair*

Bob What is the matter with you?

Teresa (*more subdued*) I don't think I can cope. I've just about had it. I don't think I can cope, any more.

Bob You do all right.

Teresa The house is in a mess. I'm in a mess. Benjamin's covered in prunes . . . Everything's foul.

Bob (*uselessly*) Never mind.

Teresa Then I read the papers and I feel more useless. Do you know that woman who raised that six hundred pounds. She's got three children.

Bob So what? She's probably got a staff of fifteen.

Teresa Three children. Here's me with one and I can't cope. And she writes letters . . .

Bob You write letters.

Teresa Nobody ever publishes mine though. I mean there must be something I can do. Something worthwhile. Instead of just sitting here, on my own, like a—cow, or something.

Pause

You're never here.

Bob I'm always here—mostly.

Teresa Not when I need you, you're not. Not when I want to talk.

They both sit gloomily in silence

Frank enters UL *carrying a small parcel done up with ribbon*

Frank (*crossing to* R *of Fiona*) Here we are. (*He puts it in front of Fiona*) There. Open your mouth, shut your eyes and prepare yourself for a big surprise. (*He hands Fiona the present*)

Fiona Oh. Thank you, darling. (*She puts the present down on table*)

Frank Well. (*He hands the present back to Fiona*) Come on, then. Open it up.

Fiona (*beginning to open the present*) Oh, all right. You do realize, I've totally forgotten to get you anything, don't you?

Frank Yes. That's all right. That's all right.

Fiona Right.

Teresa There must be someone I can help.

Bob Who?

Teresa Anyone.

Fiona (*pulling out a bottle of perfume from the parcel*) Oh. How nice.
How very nice. Thank you, darling. Very thoughtful.

Frank It's the sort you use, isn't it?

Fiona No. Not really.

Frank Oh. (*He pauses*) Oh, I see.

Fiona No, I don't usually wear this one, darling. What a lovely pretty
bottle, though, isn't it?

Frank Well, I can change it. Change it.

Fiona No, it's all right, darling. There's no need to bother. I'll just wear
it round the house. That sort of thing.

Frank Well, if you're quite sure?

Fiona (*pushing the bottle gently to one side and picking up the newspaper*)
Yes, that's quite all right, darling.

Frank (*with increasing irritation*) Had a bit of a job getting that, actually.
Couldn't remember the name you see. Had this girl in the shop opening
all the bottles, letting me have a sniff. Putting it all over herself, letting
me have a sniff, you see. Well, I felt a bit of a fool in the end. Standing
there in the middle of this big shop, sniffing away for dear life. Naturally,
you see, people were starting to stare. Stare at me sniffing. They must
have thought I had some sort of fetish, or something.

Frank stamps out UL

Fiona (*calling after him*) Thank you, darling. It was a lovely thought.
Very sweet.

Teresa jumps up and crosses to the table R *and sits at the* US *end and sorts out
paper cuttings*

Bob As a matter of fact . . .

Teresa What?

Bob Do you know who I was out with last night?

Teresa Who?

Bob William.

Teresa William who?

Bob William Featherstone.

Teresa William Featherstone? Oh him. Yes. Works in your office,
doesn't he?

Bob No. Well, same firm but different department.

Teresa Oh, I see.

Bob Yes, I was out with him.

Teresa What doing?

Bob Oh, you know. Drinking. Talking.

Teresa I didn't know he was a friend of yours?

Bob Well, no he's not really. We have a chat, now and again.

Teresa Oh. I've only met him once, haven't I? Wasn't he at that dreadful office dance?

Bob That's right.

Teresa With his wife—what's her name?

Bob Mary.

Teresa That's it. I seem to remember they were awfully boring, weren't they? What did you want to ask him out for?

Bob He asked me really.

Teresa (*rising and crossing to* L *of Bob*) Shouldn't have thought you and he had much in common.

Bob Well—we talked shop—mostly.

Teresa Till two in the morning?

Bob That and—other things.

Teresa Wish you'd talk to me till two in the morning, and other things. What else did you talk about, then?

Bob Um—oh . . .

Teresa (*snatching the paper from Bob*) I think you're making all this up. I can't believe you were out with him all that time.

Bob Well, where else do you think I was, then?

Teresa (*throwing the paper at Bob and crossing to sit* US *of the table* R) I dread to think.

Frank (*off*) Darling! Crisis! We're out of bathroom stationery.

Fiona (*with an enormous sigh, rising*) Oh dear. (*She calls*) Just a minute.

Fiona goes out UL

Bob No. If you must know—William's—a bit—upset . . .

Teresa Why?

Bob Well, it's very complicated—but—he thinks his wife is having an affair.

Teresa Mary?

Bob That's what he thinks.

Teresa I should think that's unlikely. Looking at Mary.

Bob Oh, I don't know, though . . .

Teresa She didn't look the sort to do that. Very twitchy. Can't see anyone running after her.

Bob She'd not bad looking, at all.

Teresa Oh . . .

Bob Quite attractive, in fact—to a man.

Teresa Really?

Bob Not at all bad.

Teresa Do you fancy her?

Bob Well, not personally, no. But I know a lot of people who do.

Teresa Who's she going off with, then?

Bob William doesn't know. It's all very secret, you mustn't say anything. He was very cut up about it, though.

Teresa Poor William. Oh dear. They haven't got any children, have they?

Bob No. He's a great planner is William.

Teresa Oh, well then. Did you advise him?

Bob I told him it would probably blow over.

Teresa (*rising and crossing to* L *of Bob*) Yes, that's what you usually do.

Bob What else could I say?

Teresa Well, sometimes things don't. Unless you do something positive. Sometimes you really have to do something. (*She paces and gestures* L *and* R) You can't just say—oh, Benjamin's ill, it'll blow over—the house is on fire, it'll blow over. Sometimes it isn't enough just to sit back.

Bob And what was I supposed to have done then?

Teresa He wanted advice. He came to you—God knows why—for advice.

Bob You can't advise in those sort of circumstances.

Teresa Of course you could. (*She crosses to* L *of Bob and leans over him*) If you'd been a trained marriage guidance councillor you could have done. I mean, you could have told him at least to talk to her. It may be that there's all sorts of things, that with a talk they could clear the whole thing up.

Fiona enters UL *and goes to the phone*

Bob How do you reckon Benjamin's getting on out there on his own?

Teresa Oh, I'd forgotten him. (*She hurries towards the kitchen* L) I bet he's eating the soap flakes again . . .

She goes out L

Bob smartens himself up; preparing to leave. Fiona finishes dialling. Bob's phone rings. He answers it

Bob Hallo.

Frank enters UL *and crosses to* L *of Fiona*

Fiona Just a rinse and set would be lovely . . .

Frank Darling—do you know where the . . .

Fiona (*holding her hand over receiver*) Darling, I wonder if you'd be a poppet and get the car out into the drive for me? I always ladder myself squeezing into that garage.

Frank Well, I was just looking for the screwdriver.

Fiona Bless you, darling. (*On the phone*) Hallo, yes, yes . . .

Frank crosses US

Bob Has he gone?

Fiona (*as Frank goes*) Just about.

Frank exits UL

Yes. Can you talk?

Bob Yes. Just for a second though. I'm just off to work.

Fiona No, well, I've got to be quick. Listen, do you know what last night was?

Bob Absolutely marvellous.

Fiona It was my bloody wedding anniversary.

Bob Oh, really? Congratulations.

Fiona Oh, yes, it's a scream. I feel terrible about it.

Teresa enters from the kitchen, suddenly

Teresa Bob!

Bob Yes?

Fiona What?

Teresa Do you know what that child has done with an entire jar of honey?

Bob (*into the phone*) Yes, well listen old man, I suggest your best bet is to divide the whole figure by two thirds . . .

Fiona Is she there?

Bob (*cheerfully*) Yes.

Teresa Where's the dishcloth?

Bob (*picking it up off the coffee-table and tossing it to her*) Here.

Teresa (*going*) You would not believe what that child of yours has done with an entire jar of honey.

She goes out in to the kitchen L

Bob (*into the phone*) I'm sorry, you were saying?

Fiona Listen, the point is Frank's getting rather curious as to where I was.

Bob That's funny. Same here.

Fiona What do I tell him?

Bob You were with a friend.

Fiona No. He knows practically everyone, it's too risky . . .

Bob Look, I've got to go in a minute . . .

Fiona You haven't told me what I'm going to say . . .

Bob I don't know.

Fiona What did you tell Terry, then?

Bob That I ran into someone.

Fiona Who?

Bob William Featherstone.

Fiona Who on earth is William Featherstone?

Bob He works in the Accounts Department at the office. Anyway, he's married to Mary Featherstone . . .

Fiona Oh, Lord, I remember them. What on earth made you think of them?

Bob They're safe, obscure . . . They're the first names that came into my head anyway . . .

Fiona Go on. What?

Bob Their marriage is breaking up. Third party . . .

Fiona Really, I didn't know.

Bob No, not really. That's just the story. But since it's all very hush hush nobody's to say a word . . .

Teresa (*off*) Bob—Bob—come and look at this.

Bob (*to Teresa*) Coming! (*On the phone*) Look I must go . . . Say what you like . . .

Fiona But what about . . .?

Bob puts down the phone

Teresa (*off*) Bob . . .

Bob crosses DL

Fiona Bob . . .
Bob (*going off*) What?

  Bob exits into the kitchen L

  Frank enters UL

Frank What?
Fiona (*replacing the receiver*) Oh, have you brought the car out?
Frank (*coming down the steps and crossing behind the sofa*) It's already in the drive. You didn't put it away last night.
Fiona Oh. How silly of me.
Frank No. Couple of wheels in the flower bed, actually.
Fiona (*crossing to Frank*) You must go.
Frank Yes. I was. Have you seen that screwdriver?
Fiona Screwdriver?
Frank Screwdriver. You know for screwing things. I've got to take the end off that toothbrush to get at the batteries. (*He crosses* UL *and searches in drinks cabinet*)
Fiona You don't want to do that now.
Frank Might as well do it now as later. Don't want to spend the evening sitting in the bathroom with a screwdriver. Have you put it anywhere?
Fiona (*crossing to* R *of Frank and guiding him towards kitchen* R) Have you tried the toolbox.
Frank Toolbox?
Fiona In the scullery.
Frank Oh, that toolbox. In there is it? Wondered where that had got to. Looking for a hammer only the other day.

  He goes out R

Fiona leans against door joint L *of the kitchen door* R

Fiona (*calling*) You'll have to hurry.

  Bob enters from the kitchen L *with one shoe off and clutching a blue folder and crosses to the wastepaper basket* DR

Fiona steps to R *of the sofa*

Teresa (*off*) Bob.
Bob What is it?

  Teresa comes in L *and crosses to* L *of Bob*

Teresa Bob . . . Don't you think I'm right, that if William and Mary could just get together . . .

Bob crosses DS *of the sofa searching for his shoe. Teresa follows him*

Bob Look, Terry, I'm late. Forget all about William and Mary and find my shoe.

Teresa I haven't had it.

Bob There's nothing we can do about it, it's supposed to be a dead secret, anyway.

Bob crosses US *to* C *and Teresa follows to his* R

Teresa What sort of shoe?

Bob (*pointing at his foot*) The same as this one. Only pointing the other way.

Teresa I don't know why you think I should have had it.

Teresa walks round Bob and then goes out into the kitchen L

Fiona sits on the R *arm of the sofa*

Bob (*yelling after her and crossing towards kitchen waving the file*) I think you might have had it for the same reason as you had this file of last year's estimated growth figures which I found in the breadbin. If you'd stop worrying a minute about other people and start organizing this place a bit, I think you'd be making a very valuable contribution to world peace. (*He crosses back to* C)

Teresa (*off*) It's all right, I've found it. Stop fussing.

Teresa enters from the kitchen L *and crosses to* L *of Bob holding out a brown shoe*

(*Noticing Bob is wearing a black shoe*) Oh . . .

Bob Well, it might do as a novelty . . .

Teresa I don't know where it is.

Bob Never mind. Perhaps if I walk sideways no-one will notice. (*He crosses* DR *and puts the shoe into the waste-paper basket and searches under the* L *end of the sofa*)

Teresa crosses DS *and searches under the* L *end of the sofa*

Frank enters R *with a shoe-box*

Frank Not in here. No screwdriver in here. (*He leans over the back of the sofa to show Fiona the shoe-box*)

Teresa crosses DL *and searches round the armchair*

Fiona I wouldn't imagine there would be, darling.

Frank You distinctly told me . . .

Fiona Those are the shoe brushes.

Frank Shoe brushes. What are they doing in the toolbox?

Fiona I'll show you. (*She rises and guides Frank to the kitchen door* R)

Frank and Fiona go out into the kitchen R

Bob crosses to DL *and Teresa crosses to* DRC. *Bob finds the shoe in the dolls' house* R *of the playpen*

Teresa Oh, there it is. (*She crosses to* R *of Bob*)

Bob (*sitting in the armchair* DL) How did it get in there, for crying out loud?

Teresa Oh, I think I gave it to Benjy to play with last night . . .

Bob Well, for heaven's sake, why not buy him some toys? I mean why does he have to play with—(*As Bob pulls on his shoe a strange sound comes from it. Bob puts his hand in and pulls out a toy squeaker*) What's this? (*He holds it up*)

Teresa Oh, that's his moo-moo! He loves playing farms with your shoes.

Bob (*savagely*) Well, tell him to buy his own. (*He throws the squeaker into the playpen* DL)

Teresa Honestly, the way you talk about him, sometimes, terrifies me. You're supposed to be his father . . .

Bob Terry. (*He rises and crosses to the table* DR *and collects the file*) I'm late. I am very late. Now do me a favour. During today, just go round very slowly and try and straighten up this tip, will you?

Teresa crosses to DC. *Bob crosses to* R *of Teresa*

Teresa Oh, that's lovely. Here I am, stuck in this house day after day with that kid . . .

Bob And here is five pounds. Five whole pounds. Now go mad. Go out to the nearest shop and try buying a little food. Not just jars of peanut butter—but food. (*He crosses to the door* UR *and grabs his raincoat*)

Teresa (*following to the step*) Oh go on, clear out.

Bob (*opening the front door and turning in the doorway*) And another thing, wash that child, will you? He's got enough food plastered round his face to feed a family of four.

He goes out UR *and slams the door*

Teresa crosses and puts money on the dresser UR *and then crosses* DR *and collects the phone directory from under the table*

Teresa That's right. Walk out, go on. You're no help, you're no help at all are you? (*She circles the room muttering and making ineffectual and rather violent tidying motions. She picks up the phone book, consults it, finds the number she wants, rips out the page, crosses to the phone and dials*)

Fiona enters R *and goes to the phone, dials, gets an engaged signal and irritatedly hangs up. She goes off to the hall* UL

Hallo . . . is that Mary Featherstone? Oh well, I don't know if you'll remember me, but my name is Teresa Phillips . . . Yes, that's right . . . yes. Look, Mary, this may seem a bit out of the blue, but Bob and I were wondering if you and your husband would like to come over to dinner some night . . . Well, what about tonight? . . . Oh, are you? Well, what about tomorrow, then? . . . You are? Super. Let's make it tomorrow . . . Friday . . .

Frank enters R *using a screwdriver on the toothbrush*

. . . About eight. Yes. Yes. Bye. (*She hangs up*)

She goes into the kitchen L

Fiona enters from the hall with Frank's hat, coat and umbrella

Fiona Have you done it?

Frank Not yet. One has to be careful with these things not to give oneself a shock. It's rather more sophisticated than I imagined—ah! (*The toothbrush collapses*)

Fiona (*who hasn't noticed*) Well done, darling.

Frank (*rising with the toothbrush and crossing to* UR *of the chair*) No, it appears to have come apart. Isn't that typical British workmanship? Came to pieces in my hands.

Fiona (*crossing to* L *of Frank*) Darling, you've unscrewed the wrong bit. The batteries go in there. You really are hopeless. (*Holding out his coat*) Here we are.

Frank (*struggling into his coat*) Perfectly useless. The only people who understand these things are the Japanese and they're never here when you want them. Now then. (*He takes the hat and umbrella*) Hat, umbrella, toothbrush.

Fiona You'll have to hurry.

Frank Just want to drop this in at the garage. Get them to have a look at it. Something not right with it.

Fiona Leave that now, darling. Have you got your briefcase?

Frank (*peering at the breakfast table*) Yes, it's in the—er . . . (*He crosses* DS *and picks up perfume from the table* L) If you told me the name of your stuff, I could have this changed, you see . . .

Fiona Now, do hurry, darling.

Frank Yes. (*He looks at his watch*) Good Lord, yes—Where on earth is my—er . . .

Fiona In the hall. (*She crosses* US *on to the steps* UL)

Frank (*crossing to coffee-table and picking up the* TV Times) Very good programme on the television, last night, you know. You'd have liked it.

Fiona I'll get your briefcase.

She goes out UL

Frank (*crossing to the armchair* C *and calling after her*) It was about this man who—there were two of them to start with, but one had to drop out with a pulled muscle. Anyway, this other fellow tackled it on his own. Damn near brought it off too . . .

Fiona enters UL *with Frank's briefcase*

Fiona (*handing Frank his briefcase*) Here you are.

Frank sits C *and puts the* TV Times *into his briefcase and hands Fiona the toothbrush and screwdriver*

Frank This—er—this—no, that's right. There were three of them to start with. One had the pulled muscle and the other one had—er—whatever happened to the other one? I know there was only one left in the end— Oh, he died. That's it. He died, which left only this one chap, you see . . .

Frank rises and crosses US *to the doors* UL. *Fiona follows to his* L *and kisses his cheek*

Fiona Off you go. Off you go now. Bye-bye.
Frank Yes—bye bye, darling. Lovely to have seen you.

Frank goes out UL

Fiona leans on the L *door*

Frank enters through R *door*

Whatever happened to you last night. You didn't tell me, did you?
Fiona (*crossing* DS *and picking up the perfume from the table* L) Didn't I?
Frank No. I was a bit puzzled, because I thought I heard you say earlier that you were going to that meeting, but then this Mrs—er—thing rings up and says you haven't turned up. (*He crosses to* L *of Fiona*) Got a bit worried—Didn't break down, did you? No, you can't have done —Wheels in the flowerbed.
Fiona (*with a deep breath*) No, well, actually—I decided to skip that wretched meeting for once and hurry home. I was on my way, and then —who should I run into but Mary Featherstone.
Frank Mary Featherstone? Who's Mary Featherstone?
Fiona She's William Featherstone's wife, darling. Doesn't he work with you?
Frank William Feath—oh, yes, yes—he does, indeed. How odd. Didn't know you two were friendly. That's good.
Fiona Well, we hardly—I mean hardly at all. Just one of those dreary office parties, that's the only time . . .
Frank Well, you certainly made a night of it, I must say.

Fiona crosses and sits at the R *end of the sofa and indicates that Frank should sit beside her. Frank crosses and sits* C *of the sofa*

Fiona Yes, well, the point is—Now this is terribly secret, darling, you mustn't say a word to anyone . . .
Frank What is?
Fiona Promise?
Frank Of course. What?
Fiona Well, Mary is terribly upset.
Frank Why?
Fiona I'm just telling you.
Frank I'm sorry, dear.
Fiona Putting it all in the crudest possible terms—she's pretty sure that William has another woman.
Frank Another one?
Fiona (*as to a child*) An affair, darling. A love affair.
Frank Good Lord. Good Lord. Good heavens, Featherstone?
Fiona Yes.
Frank Good grief. This is shattering.
Fiona Yes, well Mary was very upset, of course. And for some reason she chose to pour it all out to me—but you mustn't say a word darling.
Frank No, quite. Well, I must say, I'm absolutely shattered by this.
Fiona Yes. Of course, we hardly know them—but all the same . . .

Frank That's beside the point. (*He rises and crosses* L) Whether we know them or not's beside the point.

Fiona Is it? Why?

Frank Ah, well. Something you didn't know, you see. Didn't tell you. Featherstone's due to join us.

Fiona Us who?

Frank My department. All fixed. He's transferring from accounts and joining us.

Fiona (*blankly*) Oh, is he?

Frank That's the idea. Expanding you see. So he's due to join us. Key job. (*He crosses and sits in the armchair* C) He's not going to be much good if he's got all this sort of carry on—Are you sure? He seems a very quiet sort of fellow. Not the sort of chap who'd dash off the rails. Is this wife of his sure of her facts?

Fiona Well, I suppose she is, yes. (*She rises and crosses* US) I suppose she could possibly be wrong.

Frank Mind you, if she's upset enough to talk to a near stranger till God knows when in the morning . . .

Fiona (*crossing to the table* L, *putting down the perfume and picking up the tray*) Tell me, does Bob Phillips know about this appointment?

Frank Phillips, no. Why should he?

Fiona Well, I thought, seeing as he's in your department?

Frank Oh, no, no, no. Can't announce these things prematurely you know.

Fiona crosses to US *of the sofa and then exits into the kitchen* R

Board decision. (*He sees the toothbrush on the table*) That's odd. I thought I had that with me. Darling, have we got two of these things? No, no, Phillips'll be told this morning. I'm announcing it. Told Featherstone a couple of days ago, put him out of his agony, but can't start leaking things like this—not until all the candidates have been notified.

Fiona (*off*) Yes, I see.

Frank (*rising and crossing to* DC) Good Lord, I say, this is going to be very embarrassing tonight, isn't it?

Fiona (*off*) What is?

Frank I mean I had no idea at the time.

Fiona enters from the kitchen R *and crosses to* R *of Frank*

Fiona What?

Frank That the Featherstones—Oh, now I know, I know, I know—Now I know. I know what it was I was thinking last night when you didn't get back. I remember thinking—good heavens I remember thinking, I mustn't forget. I remember thinking . . .

Fiona Darling, what are you trying to say?

Frank I've invited the Featherstones to dinner.

Fiona Tonight?

Frank Yes.

Fiona Oh, that's out of the question.

Frank You're not going out are you?

Fiona Well, I may be . . .

Frank Well, can't you cancel it? Where are you going?

Fiona Um—nowhere, no. I'm not going out.

Frank Oh, that's fine. Fine. Sorry if I've caught you with your—er—guard down—lowered—but I'm sure you'll cope. Absolutely sure. Must dash. (*He kisses Fiona and crosses* US *on to the steps*) See you—er—They'll be coming about eight, by the way—Do I need a coat?

Fiona You've got one on.

Frank Yes, right. Dinner at eight—did I tell you? (*He starts out* UL)

Fiona (*dully*) Cheer-o.

Frank exits UL

Fiona crosses US *and looks at the doors and then crosses* DS *to the phone*

Teresa enters from the kitchen L *and crosses to the front door* UR *with boxes*

Fiona dials and then drops the toothbrush into the wastepaper basket. As the phone rings Teresa crosses to the table R, *drops the boxes on the table and crosses and answers phone*

Frank enters UL *and crosses to* R *of Fiona*

Frank Ah! (*He points somewhat accusingly at Fiona*)

Fiona (*hiding the phone*) What's that, darling?

Frank Toothbrush.

Fiona Mmm?

Frank Forgot the toothbrush, didn't I? Where's it gone?

Fiona There. (*She points at the wastepaper basket*) I'm afraid I threw it away.

Frank (*holding up the basket and peering in*) Ah! (*He wanders to the door still with the basket*) Caught you this time.

Teresa (*answering the phone*) Hallo.

Frank Now then, where's the—er . . .

Fiona What's the matter, darling?

Teresa Hallo?

Frank crosses to the drinks cabinet UL *and searches in the drawer. Fiona hides the phone under a cushion and crosses to* L *of Frank*

Frank Can't seem to—see it—anywhere . . .

Fiona What?

Frank doesn't reply but wanders round peering under furniture, etc

Teresa Hallo, who is that?

Frank exits into the kitchen R *and Fiona follows*

Fiona (*off*) What are you looking for?

Frank (*off*) The—thingamyjig.

Teresa Hallo. Look, if you're one of those sort of callers, you'd better hang up at once.

Frank (*off*) You haven't thrown that away, too, have you?
Fiona (*off*) Thrown what away?
Teresa I'm warning you, my husband is very strong. He's a wrestler. He has a very bad temper. And we also have dogs. Enormous dogs . . . (*She pauses to see what effect this has had*)

Frank enters from the kitchen R *and goes to the armchair* C

Fiona (*off*) Darling, what are we looking for?

Frank picks up the cushion and finds the receiver

Frank (*lifting the receiver absently to see if it's under there*) Screwdriver.
Teresa Uh? AND YOU!

Frank puts the receiver down and crosses to the table L *and sees the screwdriver on the coffee-table. Teresa puts down the phone and crosses* US

Frank Ah! It's all right, darling, I've got it. Don't panic. Got it.

Fiona enters from the kitchen R

Frank crosses to UC

Fiona Good, darling. Bye-bye now.
Frank Dinner at eight—did I tell you? Bye.

He exits UL

Fiona (*closing the doors*) Dinner at eight. Mmm.
Teresa Mmm.

Fiona and Teresa cross DS *to the coffee-table and pick up pads and pencils*

Fiona (*thoughtfully*) Avocado.
Teresa Packet of chicken noodle soup.
Fiona Courgettes.
Teresa Sprouts.
Fiona Sour cream.
Teresa Spuds.
Fiona Pork.
Teresa Chops.
Fiona Marron glacé.
Teresa Treacle pud.
Fiona Kirsch.
Teresa (*as an afterthought*) Booze!

CURTAIN

SCENE 2

The same. Evening

The set is the same as in Act I, Scene 1 except both dining-tables have been moved to UL. *The Fosters' table is parallel to the stage edge with the Phillips'*

*slightly higher table placed across it at right angles to form a "T" shape with
the top of the "T" facing* DS. *The Fosters'* C *armchair is placed* UR. *The
Fosters' trolley is* UL *of the tables. The Fosters' two dining-chairs are at the
narrow end of their table and the Phillips' two dining-chairs are at the narrow
ends of their table. There are two swivel chairs in the angles of the "T". The
three settee seats now all match the Fosters' decor*

Fiona enters from the kitchen R *with a tray of glasses and napkins. Teresa
enters from the kitchen* L *with tumblers and a packet of napkins. They
cross* DS *of dining-table. Fiona crosses to* UL *of the dining-table and puts the
tray on trolley. Teresa crosses to* UR *of her table, puts down glasses, etc., and
then crosses* US *and switches on the light* UR *and crosses back to the table.
Fiona polishes glasses and puts one at each place and then folds and lays the
napkins. Teresa places the tumblers, crosses* US *to the Welsh dresser and
empties pencils out of a glass and crosses back to the table. Teresa attempts
to fold the paper napkins, fails and pushes a napkin into each soup bowl.
They end up surveying table. Fiona* UR *of her table, Teresa* UL *of hers*

Fiona's door slams, off. She looks up. Teresa's door slams. She looks up

Frank (*off*) Darling . . .
Bob Terry . . .
Fiona In here, dear.
Teresa Hallo.

> *Frank enters* UL *crosses and kisses Fiona on the cheek, hands her a wet
> newspaper*

> *Bob enters* UR *and crosses* DS. *He carries a newspaper*

*Teresa extends her arms for an embrace. Bob passes her and crosses and sits
in the armchair* DL

Frank Hallo, darling.
Fiona (*without looking up*) Hallo.
Bob Hi!
Teresa 'Llo.
Frank Filthy night, you know. Absolutely filthy.
Fiona Pour me a drink, darling, will you? I'm dying for one.
Frank (*going to do so*) Um.

Teresa crosses to US *of Bob and puts her arms round his neck. Bob reads a
paper*

Teresa Want some tea?
Bob In a minute.
Fiona (*crossing and putting the paper on the trolley and moving the trolley to*
  DL *of her table*) You did say eight o'clock, didn't you?
Frank Er, more or less, I think.

Fiona crosses to the window, draws the curtains and then crosses to US *of the
table and switches on the light* L *of the main door. She crosses and sits at the*
R *end of the sofa*

Fiona I mean if they arrive any earlier I'm just not going to be ready, that's all.
Teresa I'll put the kettle on.

Teresa exits to the kitchen L

Bob Fine. Thank God it's Friday, that's all I can say.
Frank (*pouring sherry at the sideboard*) By George, there's been a downpour tonight. Absolutely pouring down.
Fiona I know. And that back drain's flooding again, as a result.
Frank Is it? Is it? Oh well, I'll get out there and have a poke around with a stick later on. I'll drag the old wellies out. Have a prod.
Fiona If you don't mind my saying so, I don't think your prods are awfully effective, darling. It was nearly up to the window sill last time I looked.
Frank (*crossing* DS, *handing Fiona sherry and sitting* C *of the sofa*) Here we are.
Fiona Thank you, darling. (*She drinks*) Mmmm. Lovely. You know, I don't know how I've got through today, I really don't. I must just ask you one thing, darling. If you must spring these surprise dinner parties on me, please don't do it on a Thursday again. It's one of my busiest days as it is.
Frank Well, you seem pretty busy most days to me. What's so special about Thursday?
Fiona Well, for one thing. The Thursday Guild Meeting.
Frank Oh yes, of course. I forgot that was on Thursdays, yes.
Fiona Anyway, I hope these people are going to be worth it.
Frank Oh, I should think so. He's a—he's a bright enough little fellow. Of course you know her, don't you?
Fiona Do I? Only very slightly. And remember, darling, we're not going to mention anything about that, are we?
Frank Mmmm?
Fiona About William and—er . . .
Frank Oh. Oh, good Lord, no. I'd strongly advise you not to mention it.
Fiona Fine. No confrontations, then?
Frank No need.
Fiona Just a jolly evening. How splendid. Cheers.
Frank Cheers.

They sit drinking

Bob (*rising and crossing to* DS *of his dining-table*) Terry!
Teresa (*off*) What?
Bob What's all this in aid of?
Teresa (*off*) Oh. I'll tell you. In a second.
Bob (*glaring at the table*) If you've asked your mother round . . .
Frank No, he's quite a decent sort, old Featherstone. Quite a decent sort. He has some extraordinary hobby in his spare time. Can't remember what it is. Wears boots for it. Keeps them on top of his filing cabinet . . .
Bob (*crossing to the kitchen door* L) Terry. Who is coming?

Teresa (*off*) Wait.
Frank Large boots. Don't know what he gets up to in them, though. It isn't mountaineering. I'll tell you that much.

Teresa enters from the kitchen L *with a mug of tea. She goes to* L *of Bob*

Frank rises and crosses US *to the drinks cabinet*

Teresa (*handing Bob the mug of tea*) Here we are. It is sugared.
Bob And who have you invited for dinner tonight?

Teresa crosses to the Welsh dresser for the candle and crosses to UR *of her table and puts the candle* C *of the table*

Teresa I wish you wouldn't shout. I've only just this minute got Benjamin off to sleep.
Bob (*quietly; crossing to* UL *of his table*) I am asking you—who?
Frank And it wasn't rock-climbing, either . . .
Teresa Well—the Featherstones, actually.

Teresa exits into the kitchen L

Bob (*after a pause*) I see . . . (*He sits* US *of the table*)
Frank (*crossing to* L *of the sofa*) I'll tell you something else though. Whatever he gets up to in these boots of his, he doesn't take his wife. I know that. Goes off on his own. Which either means that it's dangerous. Or else—or else it's tied up with this other business. That's a point . . . (*He ponders, then crosses* US *to the drinks cabinet*)

Teresa enters from the kitchen L *and crosses to* L *of the table and picks up the packet of napkins*

Bob And what exactly do you intend to do? Sort out their marriage over dinner?
Teresa Of course not.
Bob Well?
Teresa If friends need help . . .
Bob They will ask for it. Exactly. When did you decide to ask them round here?
Teresa Yesterday morning. After you'd told me.
Bob I see. And now we have to sit through a whole evening of them, do we? We have to put up with the most excruciating evening, just because you have nothing better to do with your time.
Teresa I have plenty of other——
Bob Then mind your own business.
Teresa If you had a scrap of sensitivity——
Bob I'm sensitive enough to know when people want to be left alone.
Teresa Well. It's too late now, isn't it. They're coming.

Teresa exits into the kitchen L

Frank (*crossing to* UL *of the sofa*) Do you think this is a possibility? He uses those boots of his to tramp off and see this other woman of his. Perhaps she lives on a marsh, or something. Which would explain why he keeps them in the office. He doesn't want his wife to see them. You see?

Fiona (*rising and crossing to* UR *of the sofa*) Darling. I do wish you'd look at that drain, before too long. And I must get ready. I seem to remember they were awfully sombre people. I do hope they won't be too impossible.

Frank Good Lord, no. What did you think of my theory about those boots of his, by the way?

Fiona Well, I suppose it's feasible, darling. But I do think it's a trifle oblique. (*She starts to go*)

Frank Yes, I'd better go and look out that stick for the drain. You haven't moved it, I hope.

Fiona crosses to the kitchen doorway R. *Frank starts to follow, but she indicates that he go the other way*

Fiona No, it's round the back, behind the garage, I think. I should go out the front door and round that way. It's ankle deep in the yard.

Fiona exits into the kitchen R

Frank (*crossing to double doors*) Yes. Right. Well, throw me a line if I— oh, never mind.

Frank exits UL

Teresa enters from the kitchen L *switches on the light* L *of the kitchen door, and then crosses to the window* R

Bob (*rising*) Well, if I'm expected to spend an evening with those two, I'm entitled to a drink.

Teresa I've bought some.

Bob Where?

Teresa (*drawing the curtains* R *and pointing to a bottle of white wine on the table*) There.

Bob (*studying the bottle disgustedly*) Oh my God.

Teresa (*alarmed*) It's not South African, is it?

Bob (*crossing to the front door* UR) I'm going out now.

Teresa (*crossing to* L *of Bob*) You can't!

Bob I can!

Teresa How long for?

Bob A bit.

Bob goes out UR

Teresa Bob . . .

Bob (*off, shouting back*) It depends . . .

Teresa Bob!

Teresa stands for a moment, undecided. Then, impetuously she snatches a coat from the pegs near the UR *door, hurries to the other door* L *and listens a moment for Benjamin. Seemingly all is well for after a second she*

dashes out of the front door in pursuit of Bob. She pulls the door to but does not latch it

The stage is empty for a second. Silence. Both doorbells ring. A pause. They ring again

William peers round the double doors UL. *Mary peers around front door* UR. *A few moments then William and Mary enter, both in their thirties. He carries a hat and wears a soaking wet mac and enters through Fiona's front door. She, although in a coat, is bone dry. She enters through Teresa's door*

William (*calling*) Hallo . . .
Mary (*calling*) Hallo . . .

William and Mary move cautiously and cross DS *meeting* UC. *They look at each other*

William Nobody here.
Mary Funny.
William Very odd.
Mary (*anxiously*) We're not early are we?
William Of course we're not.
Mary (*calling off one way*) Hallo!
William No, don't do that. Don't do that.
Mary Let them know we're here.
William Well, we can just wait quietly. Don't have to shout about. They'll be here when they're ready, I expect . . .
Mary Table's laid.
William Oh yes?
Mary (*nervously laughing*) We're expected, anyway.
William Yes, well we would be.
Mary (*wandering* R *and back to* R *of William, nibbling her nails*) Oh—I feel awful just, walking into their house. I——
William Now don't start to get nervous. There's nothing at all to get nervous about. Just keep calm. (*He takes her hand from her mouth and smacks it like he would a child's*) Sit down if you want to.
Mary No, I won't sit down—I . . .
William Did you take your tablets?
Mary Yes . . .

William puts his arm round Mary and then crosses to DL *of Fiona's table*

William Good. Now you just have to be natural. No need to put on any act. No need at all. Just be yourself.
Mary Yes. It's just I—never—seem to be able to say anything.
William You don't have to if you don't want to. Nobody's asking you to say anything unless you feel you want to.
Mary But if I don't I feel so—so . . .

Fiona enters from the kitchen R

Fiona Darling, I . . .

Mary hides behind William. William steps forward

(*Crossing* DS *to William*) Oh, Good Lord. You're here. Hallo.

William Hallo. Sorry to surprise you, but we rang a couple of times—didn't get a reply—and the door was off the latch, so we . . .

Fiona Oh, well. Good heavens, yes, very sensible of you. Frank must have left it open. He's having a go at our drains . . . Good heavens, let me take your coat. You're soaked.

William Quite a downpour.

Fiona Yes. What a downpour.

William turns to take his coat off. Fiona crosses to R of Mary, who backs away

And how are you, Mary?

Mary (*inaudibly*) Oh. Fine, thank you.

Fiona Mmmm?

William She's had a bit of a cold, haven't you, Mary, but I think she's over it now.

Fiona Oh, I'm sorry to hear that. (*She takes William's coat*) I'll just pop that in the hall, let it dry out, then we can all have a sherry.

Fiona crosses and exits UL

William (*crossing to* R *of the table holding out his hat*) Very charming, isn't she? Very charming woman.

Mary (*in an undertone, crossing to* UL *of the table*) I don't like sherry.

William (*crossing* US *of the sofa*) Well, just ask for a small glass, then.

Mary But it gives me terrible indigestion.

William (*crossing to* R *of the sofa*) Well, say you'd like a cream sherry. You liked the cream sherry we had at Bertha's at Christmas.

Mary No, I didn't. Bertha just kept giving it to me. I didn't like it at all. Shall I ask if I can have a tonic water?

William You can't ask her for a tonic water. People don't drink tonic water. Not for an hors d'oeuvres . . .

Mary (*desperately*) Well, what shall I say?

Fiona enters UL *and crosses to drinks cabinet*

William hides his hat under the sofa cushion R

Fiona I've put it just by the radiator. Should be dry in no time. Now then what are we all having? Mary?

Mary Um . . .

Fiona What would you like?

Mary Er . . .

Fiona Sherry?

Mary Well I . . .

Fiona Medium? Or would you prefer dry?

Mary Thank you very much.

Fiona Dry. William?
William Same again, please.
Fiona Three dry. Jolly good. (*She pours the sherry*)
William Very nice room.
Fiona Thank you.
William Very nice indeed. Very tasteful.
Fiona Here we are, Mary. (*She crosses to Mary with the sherry*)

Mary goes to take the sherry and finds she is wearing her gloves. She pulls them off and takes the sherry. Fiona crosses back to the drinks cabinet and takes two sherries and crosses and hands William a sherry. Mary crosses DSL *to* R *of Bob's armchair*

Fiona Well, I suppose we drink to your new job, William.
William Well, thank you.
Fiona Cheers, then.
William Good health.

They drink. Mary coughs

Fiona Oh, dear. All right?
Mary Thank you. All right. (*She hiccups*)
Fiona Yes, Frank's absolutely delighted you're joining the department. He speaks awfully highly of you. Awfully highly.
William Pleased to hear it.
Fiona You're absolutely wizard with figures apparently?
William Yes, well I've always been interested in them.

Mary hiccups

Seemed to come naturally . . .
Fiona In that case, I think you're awfully clever. I'm afraid I'm hopeless. I can't even add up the shopping list. Then I'm afraid that's just women, isn't it?

Mary hiccups

William Yes, I'm afraid you're right, there. I have to keep a firm eye on Mary's accounts, don't I, Mary?
Fiona Lucky you, Mary.
Mary (*smiling*) Yes. (*She hiccups and attempts to stifle them*)

A silence

Fiona And what have you both been up to? Anything exciting?
William No, no.
Fiona Oh. Well, it's been pretty dull all round for everyone, hasn't it? (*She pauses*) I mean, I always think these things go in phases, don't they. You have an exciting bit of the year. And then all of a sudden you get a dull bit of the year. (*She pauses*) I don't know why that should be, at all, do you? But I've always found that, for some reason. (*She pauses*) Must be to do with the time of year I suppose. In the summer you can always get out, can't you? But then when you come to winter, on a day like today, and you can't do anything really. You're just stuck indoors all day. Wishing you could get out. Only you can't. You have to sit

indoors, waiting till the dreary old weather gets brighter again. (*She pauses*) Look, I think I really ought to dash out and drag Frank in. (*She crosses and puts her glass on the drinks cabinet*) Not fair for him to miss all the fun, is it?

Fiona exits UL

William and Mary cross US. *William to* DR *of the steps and Mary to* UL *of the table*

Mary She's very elegant, isn't she?
William Oh, well. She's used to this sort of thing.

Mary puts her glass on the table

(*Crossing to* R *of Mary*) Mr Foster must give dozens of these sort of informal dinner parties. She'll be used to entertaining people.
Mary I don't think I could ever . . . (*She starts to nibble her nails again*)
William Oh, yes you will. Yes you will. You'll see. (*He smacks Mary's hand*) We'll have to start doing this sort of thing soon, you know.
Mary Oh, I hope we don't . . . (*She crosses towards the window* L)
William (*crossing* US *to the drinks cabinet and putting down his glass*) Well, people will expect it, you see. You can't just accept entertainment and not give it, can you. No need to worry. You'll soon find yourself enjoying these sort of things as much as she does, you'll see.

Teresa's doorbell rings

Mary (*after a nervous pause*) What was that?
William The bell.

The bell rings again

Mary Who is it?
William Somebody wanting to get in.
Mary Who?
William I don't know. Go and have a look.
Mary Do you think I should?
William Go on.

They stand either side of the door UR. *Mary opens it gingerly*

Teresa is revealed

Teresa Hallo.
William Hallo, Terry.
Mary Hallo.
Teresa (*awkwardly*) You're here. This is very unusual—the guests letting the hostess in.
William Very unusual.
Mary That's all right.
William We rang the bell. But we thought you must have all died.
Teresa No—actually—Bob's out—at the moment. He's just popped out. And I've been out, too, getting some air . . . Forgot my key. Will you

excuse me? I must just see to Benjamin. (*She moves to the kitchen door* L)

Mary How is he?

Teresa Oh. Big. Fat. Spoilt.

Mary (*dismayed*) Ah.

Teresa No, actually he's super, but we don't tell him that or he'll get conceited, like his father.

Teresa goes out to the bedroom L

William Are you sure you got the telephone message right?

Mary How do you mean?

William She doesn't exactly look ready to entertain.

Mary Yes, Friday night. I remember. She wanted us to come last night only we couldn't because we had to go to the Fosters'.

Teresa enters holding a wet nappy

Teresa Sorry. (*To Mary*) Take your coat, shall I?

Mary Thank you. (*She fumbles out of her coat*)

Teresa, needing two hands to help her, hands William the wet nappy. He takes it inadvertently. Mary removes her coat revealing a fairly awful dress. Teresa takes the coat and moves up to the door UR *to hang it up. William notices that Mary is still wearing her cardigan*

William (*urgently*) Cardigan!

Mary What?

William Take off your cardigan.

Mary whips it off and tucks it under her arm to conceal it. Teresa rejoins them having taken a fresh nappy from a pile by the door UR

Teresa (*noticing Mary's dress for the first time*) Oh. That's lovely . . . (*She sees she has left William holding the nappy*) Oh, sorry. (*She takes the nappy from William*)

Teresa goes off into the kitchen L

William (*taking the cardigan from Mary and going to hang it up*) I think I'd better wash my . . . (*Seeing Teresa has gone he wipes his hands on his handkerchief*)

Teresa (*off*) Well, at least the weather's better than last night. Wasn't it terrible?

Mary Yes, we were caught in it.

Teresa (*off*) Were you?

Teresa enters

Oh yes, how did that go?

William What's that?

Teresa Your dinner with the big man. How did it go?

William Very pleasant. Very pleasant indeed.

Teresa Yes, isn't Frank the sweetest old thing?

Mary Oh, yes, I thought Mr Foster was very nice indeed . . .

Teresa And how was the fabulous Fiona?

William Charming. I found her very charming indeed.

Teresa Yes, she's certainly that. What did you think, Mary? Had you met her before?

Mary Only once. At the party. I thought she was quite—nice.

Teresa Yes. I think she gets on better with the men. I'm sorry. I think she's a bitch. (*She crosses to the kitchen doorway*)

William Oh, come now . . .

Mary crosses to R of Teresa. William crosses to her L

Mary Can I have a peep at Benjamin later on?

Teresa Yes, can you wait until he's gone off properly? Otherwise he'll be up all through dinner. I know him.

Mary All right.

Teresa Would you excuse me a minute? I must just finish seeing to him. Sit down. Make yourselves comfy.

Teresa exits the kitchen L

William and Mary turn and face DS. Mary crosses and sits in the armchair DL. William crosses DS and wanders R and L

William Sit, sit, sit. They could really make this room into something, if they put their minds to it.

Mary I think Terry's looking awfully tired . . .

William Get it all repapered, lick of paint—make a proper difference that would . . .

Mary I wonder where Bob's gone?

William Gone out, didn't she say?

Mary That's what she said. I wonder why she invited us round?

William For a meal.

Mary Never has before. We hardly know her really . . .

William (*crossing to R of Mary*) I shall be working at the next desk to him, now.

Mary It wasn't him who invited us, it was her.

William I don't know what you're going on about, I'm sure. (*He crosses US, picks up the glass from Fiona's drinks cabinet and crosses to DS of the steps. He is pacing up and down, jigging about—he whistles to himself*)

Mary rises, crosses US, picks up her glass from the table and crosses to L of William

Mary What's the matter?

William Matter?

Mary Why are you—?

William Nothing. Nothing at all. (*He paces a bit more*) Just wondering where the—whereabouts their—that's all.

Mary Upstairs?

William Probably. And downstairs, I wouldn't be surprised.

Mary (*impressed*) Two?
William In a house like this—knowing Mr Foster—almost bound to.

Frank enters from the kitchen R, pauses and turns in doorway. He is without his shoes

Frank Ah! Hallo there—darling, I thought you said Pinky and Perky had arrived . . .

William breaks DS. Frank crosses DS, R of the sofa. William crosses DS, L of the sofa and Mary follows to L of William

William Oh, hallo, Mr Foster. Have you met my wife, Mary—Mr Foster.
Mary How do you do.
Frank Yes, of course we've met. One of those—er do's. Office do's.
Mary Fancy remembering.
Frank Ah, well now. That's me you see. Always remember the—er good looking women never their bloomin' husbands . . .

William and Mary laugh politely

Matter of fact. Let you into a secret. Everyone thinks that I promoted your husband because he's the best man at his job. But that's not the real reason.

Mary hides behind William

After his lovely wife, actually. (*He crosses DS of William and Mary and then US to the drinks cabinet*)

William pushes Mary US and follows to her R

Both drinking are you? Think I'll join you. Been out in all this, poking about in the drains, for my sins. Have to excuse my socks—no shoes. Point is, changed into my boots—(*with a sudden sharp, significant look at William*)—boots, did my bit with the stick out there, got back in here, someone'd pinched my shoes . . .
William Stolen them?
Frank Well, probably not stolen. More—moved them, perhaps.
Mary I'm always losing things.
Frank Are you? (*He crosses to L of Mary*) Same as me.
William I'm always having to go round finding things for her.
Frank So's my wife. Gets absolutely hopping mad. Fill you up, can I?
William Thank you.
Frank Mary?
Mary No, I think I've . . .
Frank Haven't drunk that yet, have you? Want something else? Whisky, gin, Martini?
Mary No thank you, I . . .
Frank What else have we got? (*He crosses to the drinks cabinet and looks in cupboard*)
William (*jigging up and down again*) Excuse me—I wonder if I could just . . .

Frank Yes, yes, of course. (*He crosses to Mary and indicates the sofa*)

Mary crosses and sits C of the sofa and William sits at L end

(*Crossing back to the drinks cabinet*) Sit down. Take a seat. Now then. Let's see. Orange juice, ginger ale, soda water, tonic water . . .

Mary jumps up. William follows

Mary Oh, well . . .
Frank Tonic water?

William pulls Mary down and they sit

Mary Thank you.
Frank Jolly good. (*He opens a bottle of tonic*)
William We were just saying, what a nice room this is?
Frank Room?
William Yes.
Frank Yes, I suppose it is. I've seen it before of course. (*He crosses to L of the sofa with the drinks*) Here we are. Jolly good health.
William Cheers.
Mary Thank you.

Frank gestures to William and Mary to move up, which they do, and Frank sits at the L end of the sofa

Frank You know, I'd just like to say this to you both and—er you can take this as you like. My wife and I—we've been married—well, it was our anniversary yesterday—for God knows how many years. And there are times when acrimony creeps in. That is to say—we both get on each other's wick. Now then, what I always say to myself at times likes these is well, Frank, it's better than nothing. And the older you get the better it is and the bigger the nothing. So my advice is, stick it out. Stick it out. Don't do things now that you're going to regret when you get too old, like me, to want to do them any more. (*He pauses*) And that's all I have to say on the matter. Cheers!

William⎫
          ⎬(*together*) Cheers!
Mary ⎭

Fiona enters from the kitchen R and crosses to L of the sofa

William and Mary rise. William sits and pulls Mary down

Fiona Oh, hallo, is Frank looking after you all right? Dinner won't be long.
Frank Ah, that's good news. All getting a bit peckish, I think, aren't we? I certainly am.
Fiona Good. Darling, you left your shoes on top of the stove. I thought you might need them. (*She hands Frank his shoes*)
Frank Ah!
Fiona What have you all been talking about, then? Anything interesting?
Frank (*significantly to William and Mary*) No, no, no—just er chatting.

Fiona (*loathe to leave them*) Chatting—? Well—yes . . . Won't be too long now.

Fiona exits into the kitchen R

William rises. Mary rises. William sits. Mary sits. William rises

Frank Um.

William (*hopping up and down a bit*) Excuse me. Do you think I could just pop up and wash my hands?

Frank Oh, yes of course. (*He pulls William down*) I'd better give you the directions. Better explain the geography to you. (*He pulls on a shoe, and places it on the drinks table to tie up the lace*)

William moves the glasses to make more room, and Frank misinterprets the gesture and thinks that William is offering to do the lace up

Oh, that's very kind of you—just a loose bow. Well, you go up one flight, there's a door on your left. Pass that. Then you pass the door that's straight ahead of you as well. Now after that, if you sort of follow the passage which tends to double back on itself, if you see what I mean, the second door on your left, after you've turned that corner, is the bathroom. Ready for the other one, are you? (*He puts the other foot on the table*) If you want the other thing, it's nearly obliquely opposite it, on your right, as it were.

William Yes. Thank you. (*He rises*)

Frank (*pulling William down*) It's a bit of a brute to pull, by the way. If it doesn't go first time, don't get into a flap. The trick is—give a sharp, firm yank—count a slow seven and then bash the cistern with the palm of your hand, just to the left of the name plate. You can't miss.

William Right.

Frank Have a good time.

William Right.

William rises and exits rapidly UL

Frank looks at Mary. She reacts nervously. He moves to C *of the sofa, next to Mary*

Frank A lot of men get up to this sort of thing, you know. But it blows over.

Mary Does it?

Frank Almost invariably.

Mary What does?

Frank If you're in any sort of trouble at all—you know the sort of trouble I mean—please feel that you can come and chat it over with me, or my wife. I won't try and pretend that William isn't going to be a great asset to our department. And it's my job, in so far as it's possible, to see he's happy. But I think that includes you.

Mary Thank you.

Frank My wife put me in the picture about you, you see.

Mary Did she?

Frank Oh yes. We don't have any secrets between us. She told me all about your little meeting.
Mary What meeting?
Frank Last night.
Mary I didn't go to any meeting.
Frank No, no, no. Your meeting with her.
Mary I was at home all last night. William was away you see . . .
Frank Home?
Mary Watching television.
Frank Oh, were you? That's odd—I thought my wife said she—Oh, television? Ah, you didn't happen to see that programme about these three chaps . . .
Mary Oh—yes, peculiar wasn't it?

William enters UL

William (*crossing to* L *of the sofa*) Found it first go.
Frank Oh, well done.
William While I was in there, I—er—took the liberty of easing the pin on your ball-cock.
Frank Well. As long as you enjoyed yourself. (*He rises to* R *of William*) Look, I'll just nip into the kitchen now and see if the wife wants a hand. (*He pushes William on to the sofa and crosses to* US *of the sofa*) You two feel perfectly free to—talk. You're a couple of sillies. I've a jolly good mind to bang your heads together. (*He bangs their heads together*)

Frank goes out R, *laughing*

Mary (*rising and crossing to* R *of William*) William . . .
William Yes?
Mary Mr Foster was just saying something very peculiar.
William What sort of thing?
Mary Well, I don't know, but he seemed to be saying . . .
William Now what?
Mary No, it's silly. (*She nibbles her nails*)
William I'm afraid you're being more incoherent than usual tonight, Mary. (*He crosses to* DS *of the kitchen door* L)

Mary crosses to his R

I'm not following you at all. (*He goes to smack her hand*)

Teresa enters L

William changes the movement into a gesture of greeting. Teresa crosses to US *of her dining-table*

Teresa Hallo. I've been—trying to get everything ready. I don't know what's happened to Bob, I'm sure.
Mary Can we help?
Teresa Well, no, I think I've done most of it now, thanks. Oh, I tell you what. If you're feeling strong, William, I wonder if you'd . . . (*She holds out the wine*)

William (*crossing* D *of the table and taking the bottle*) Yes, of course. (*He crosses to* R *of the dining-table with the bottle and corkscrew and tries to draw the cork*)

Mary Got Benjamin off to sleep have you?

Teresa Oh yes, he's all right. Not a sound. Want to have a peep at him?

Mary Oh, could I? I'll be very quiet.

Teresa It's all right. Once he's off, he's off. Through the kitchen and—oh, you'll find it.

Mary (*going*) Right.

Mary crosses to the kitchen doorway L *and exits into the kitchen*

Teresa (*crossing to* UL *of William and tapping him on the shoulder*) Can you manage?

William Oh yes. Yes, I've opened one or two in my time, I can tell you.

Teresa Yes. (*She pauses. She crosses and sits on* DS *end of her dining-table with her feet on the chair*) I suppose that's where Bob is.

William Where?

Teresa In the pub.

William Oh well, he might be. I've heard he enjoyed a drink. He's usually in the pub with that crowd from the office at lunchtimes. I've seen them all going in. (*He draws the cork and hands corkscrew to Teresa and crosses to her* R)

Teresa (*taking the bottle from him and putting it back on the table*) You don't drink at lunchtimes, then?

William Oh no. I'd be fast asleep. No, as a matter of fact, I drink very sparingly, altogether.

Teresa (*smiling*) How did you survive with Bob the other night, then?

William Other night?

Teresa On that binge you both had?

William Binge? When was this?

Teresa Couple of nights ago. When was it? Wednesday.

William Not Wednesday. I was in Scunthorpe on Wednesday.

Teresa Scunthorpe?

William Yes. First Wednesday of every month. Always the same. Stay the night there. Visit our branch, look over their books. Don't know why it should be Wednesday, though, I'm sure. Always has been.

Teresa Scunthorpe?

William Yes. Anything wrong?

Teresa Have you ever been out for a drink with Bob?

William No. I said, I wasn't the drinking . . .

Teresa Have you ever—discussed your marriage with Bob at all?

William Discussed it, how do you mean?

Teresa Talked to him about it, in detail, you know what I mean.

William Certainly not, no. I don't believe in——

Teresa (*dangerously quiet*) Thank you. That's all I want to know. Thank you. (*She begins to stack Bob's cutlery and crockery back on to the tray*) Well . . .

William watches fascinated as Teresa walks past him carrying the tray, opens the front door and tosses it fully laden, almost casually, into the street. She closes the door

William Terry, what are you doing?

Teresa Would you pour me a drink please?

William Yes. Of course. (*He does so*)

Teresa Well—that's it. As far as I'm concerned that's it.

William What's it?

Teresa That—is—it. (*She takes a wine glass that William has poured*) Up his! (*She drains the glass*)

William Steady on.

Teresa I'm going to get the supper. (*She crosses L of the table, US of the table and then to R of William*)

William backs away DL

(*Following William*) I'm going to be absolutely madly, permissively modern. I am going to serve up the food and then, in the absence of our lord and master, who is probably grovelling on the floor with some barmaid by now, we will all sit down and have a lovely chatty meal.

William sits DL

(*Crossing US*) That's what.

Mary enters from the kitchen L

Mary Isn't he beautiful?

Teresa (*hostilely*) Who's beautiful?

Mary Benjamin.

Teresa and Mary cross DS

He's the dead spit of Bob, isn't he? Just like his daddy.

Teresa Oh yes. The same squat, piggy little face, you mean.

Mary Oh no, I didn't.

Teresa Same nature, too, you know. Screams for what he wants till he gets it. He'll be a real little charmer when he grows up.

Mary sits on the R arm of the chair DL

Just like his bloody father . . .

Teresa goes out L

Mary What's wrong?

William Something very wrong, I'm afraid.

Mary What?

William I don't know. Something to do with Scunthorpe.

Mary Scunthorpe?

William And Bob's drinking. Then she threw a load of cutlery out of the front door . . .

Mary Perhaps the dinner's spoilt.

William No. I rather think it's something more than that, somehow.
Mary Oh.

Fiona enters R with a tray containing four dishes of avocado

Fiona At last. You must have thought we'd gone to bed or something. (*She crosses to R of the dining-table and puts down the dishes*) Now, I've put you, Mary, there. And William here. (*She puts the tray on the trolley*)

William and Mary cross each other DS and cross to chairs US of Fiona's dining-table. Mary sits UR of the table. William crosses and holds Fiona's chair out for her. Fiona sits at the end of the table. Mary jumps up and sits again. William sits R of Fiona

Do sit down. Frank's just digging us up something to drink from somewhere.

William and Mary both sit on swivel chairs which can swing through ninety degrees to take in Bob and Teresa's section as well

Now, I hope you like avocado. I know some people loathe them. (*She serves the dishes to all four*) Now this is all going to be terribly informal, so please don't expect anything elaborate. If I've forgotten to give you anything just yell out. At the rate Frank's going he'll probably join us for coffee, but please do start.

Teresa enters with a tureen of soup

William and Mary swivel round. William rises

Teresa It's all right. Don't get up.
Mary Can we help?
Teresa No. No, it's all right. I can manage perfectly, thank you. Just about. Everything's under control. I think. Just help yourselves—please help yourselves. Can you smell burning? (*She sniffs*)
William Er . . .
Teresa (*rushing out*) I knew it. I knew it.

Teresa goes off into the kitchen L

Mary (*after a pause, starting to serve the soup*) Soup, William?
William (*taking a bowl*) Thank you. (*He sniffs the soup*)
Mary What are you doing?
William It smells of air freshener.
Mary No.
William Definitely air freshener.
Mary Well, try and eat it. She's gone to a lot of trouble.
William You know what happens to my stomach with badly cooked food.
Mary Yes, dear. I know.

Frank enters R with an opened bottle of wine

William and Mary swivel

Frank Whoever put this cork in, did a good job. Been dancing round the
kitchen trying to get it out.
Fiona Sit down, darling.
Frank Right. (*He sits*) Ah. Now then. What's this stuff?
Fiona Avocado, you've had it before.
Frank Yes, I know I've had it before. Didn't recognize it that's all. Is it
all right?
William Delicious.
Mary Mmmm.
Frank Looks a bit off to me.
Fiona Darling . . .
Frank Now then. (*He rises*) Wine everybody? Mary?
Mary Oh, no, thank you.
Frank (*pouring her some all the same*) Oh, come on . . .

Teresa enters from the kitchen L

William and Mary swivel

Teresa That stove. That damned stove. I have asked Bob a hundred times
—well I'm not waiting for him. He can damn well starve.

Frank crosses to pour Fiona's wine

Mary Is there anything the matter, Terry?
Teresa Matter? Matter? Good heavens no. Come on then. Let's enjoy
ourselves. Eat up . . .
Mary Right. This looks delicious. (*She picks up her spoon*)

William continues to gaze at his plate, dubiously

Teresa William?
William Er—yes, thank you . . .

William and Mary swivel

Frank (*offering William wine*) William?
William Thank you.

William and Mary swivel

Teresa I hope you enjoy this soup. I stood over it for hours.

William and Mary dip their spoons in the soup

I've put practically everything in it I could lay my hands on.

William and Mary each take a mouthful

Benjie helped me with it a little bit.

William and Mary choke

Mary (*recovering*) Aren't you having any?
Teresa I couldn't face it just at the moment. Don't mind me. I'll just get
drunk.

William and Mary swivel. Frank sits

Frank This doesn't taste like avocado at all to me. Tastes like pineapple chunks.

Fiona If you're going to complain, darling, the best thing to do is not to eat it.

Frank I'm not complaining. I prefer pineapple chunks, actually.

William and Mary swivel

Teresa How is it?

Mary Wonderful.

William Very unusual.

Teresa (*picking up the ladle*) I can't resist it. I'll have to try it. (*She sips the soup, replaces the ladle and stares at it*) It tastes like anti-perspirant.

Mary Oh.

William Well . . .

Teresa Doesn't it taste like that to you? It must do.

Mary No . . .

William Yes, it does.

Teresa Then what the hell are you eating it for, for God's sake? Here, let me pour it back. (*She snatches their plates*)

Mary (*resisting*) No, it's . . .

Teresa Give it to me.

A tug of war

Come on. (*She gets their plates and pours the soup back into the tureen*) Well that's that. End of the meal.

William Oh? Why is that?

Teresa The chops are completely burnt and I don't know how you feel about raw potatoes.

William Ah.

Mary Oh dear.

Teresa (*cheerfully*) Never mind. There's always the wine, isn't there? The least we can do is behave like civilized human beings. I don't know about you two but I'm going to enjoy myself. (*She starts to sing loudly and discordantly*)

William and Mary sit appalled till she finishes and takes another swig of wine. William and Mary swivel

Frank What have we got coming up after this then?

Fiona Frigadella.

Frank Frigadella? Frozen stuff, eh?

Fiona No, darling, it's veal and pork.

Frank Oh, well, I expect we'll recognize it when we see it. Talking of recognizing things, we had a little chap in the office once. Came from somewhere up North. Perkins was it? No, it was Porter—Porterhouse. Some name like that.

Fiona Darling, do eat.

Frank No, it was Carter. That's it. Billy Carter. Don't know where I got the name Porterhouse from. Anyway he came from up North. He had the most terrible wife. Little woman. Now in those days the Chairman was very keen to make it one big happy family. And that included the wives. Now it was just before the office Christmas party and he decided to put Mrs Carter in charge of the—no, it wasn't Carter. What was her name now . . .?

Fiona Darling, we are all simply panting for our second course.

William and Mary swivel

Teresa Did you ever hear that very funny story about the wife who came home unexpectedly and found her husband in bed with the baby-sitter.

Mary Oh!

William No I don't believe we have.

Teresa Well, there they both were, you see. Him and this girl——

William Terry, I wonder if I could just——

Teresa Both of them on the bed. At it for dear life——

The doorbell rings

—and the wife just stands there and says——

William Isn't that the doorbell?

Teresa The wife says—let it ring—says to her husband very sweetly——

William I think that was the doorbell.

Teresa (*sharply*) Let it ring—she says to him, terribly sweetly, "You can practise till you're blue in the face, darling, but you'll never get it right."

Mary laughs nervously

William (*appalled*) Mary!

Mary stops laughing. William and Mary swivel

Frank (*slamming down his spoon, having suddenly remembered*) Fraser! That was it. Mrs Fraser.

Fiona Well done, darling. I'll get the rest. (*She rises and picks up the tray from trolley*)

Mary also rises

No, sit still Mary. I can manage.

Frank Anyway, now then. Mrs—I've forgotten what I was telling you about now.

William The office Christmas party.

Frank Oh yes. And Mrs——

Mary Mrs Carter.

Frank Carter? That wasn't her name.

William Mrs Fraser.

Frank Fraser! That's it, Fraser. Yes, the Chairman decided to put Mrs— I don't think that was her name either, come to think of it. What was it now?

Fiona (*going out with the plates*) Darling, you really are becoming awfully tedious.

Fiona goes out to the kitchen R

As she does so Teresa's doorbell rings. William and Mary swivel

William (*rising*) I think I'd better answer it.
Teresa It's entirely up to you, Bill. I'm not answering anything. I'm going to enjoy my dinner.

Frank polishes his cutlery thoughtfully on the tablecloth. Bob's singing is heard off

William opens the door and recoils as Bob lunges in holding a carrier bag

Bob Well, well, all tucking in are we? Filling ourselves with goodies? Very nice too. Did you cook anything for me, love, or shall I go the Café?
Teresa Oh God!
Bob Hallo, there's Mary the mouse. Hallo, Mary the mouse, how are you?
Mary Hallo—Bob . . .
Bob Well, then. How have things been going? (*He shoves William*) Sit down, William, don't mind me . . .

William does so

All been telling dirty jokes, have we?
Teresa Yes. I've heard some very dirty jokes, thank you.
Bob I thought you might. I thought you'd soon ferret that out.
Teresa Well I did.
Bob Good. (*He turns his attention to the carrier bag*) Now then, what have we here? (*He starts to unload a number of tins of beer*)

William and Mary swivel

Fiona enters from the kitchen R *with two vegetable dishes*

Fiona First batch. (*She puts the dishes down on the table*)
William Sure you can manage?
Fiona Yes, thank you. Frank will give me a hand. Won't you, darling?
Frank What? Oh yes. You should have said. Should have said.
Fiona It's fairly obvious, darling. I don't have to tell you, surely? You can see me, staggering in and out laden with dishes.

Frank and Fiona go out to the kitchen R

William and Mary swivel

Bob (*opening a can of beer and crossing to* L *of Teresa*) Who's for beer then? Eh? William, I know you'll have one?
William Er, no thanks, Bob. Got the wine, thank you.
Bob (*aggressively*) Come on. Have a beer. (*He pours beer into William's glass*)

William covers the glass with his hand

Teresa Bob, we're having a meal. Either sit down or——
Bob (*crossing to* R *of Teresa*) Mary. Mary will have a beer. Won't you, Mary?

Mary Oh, no, no—thanks . . .
Bob Well, she won't. (*He nods at Teresa*) She thinks beer's a bit common actually. You know what she likes? Egg Nog. Egg Nog—known as alcoholic custard.
Teresa Bob, shut up.
Bob Why should I shut up? I'm offering our friends a drink, that's all. (*He leans over Mary*) Do excuse her manners. Her education was not what it should have been.
Teresa (*dangerously quiet*) I warn you, I shall throw something.
Bob Oh, that'll be good. They'll enjoy that. (*He crosses to* US *of William*) She's got a good aim. Hit a wall with a plate of baked beans at twenty paces. (*He swings a beer can over Willaim's head*)

William ducks

(*Crossing to* DL *of the dining-table*) You don't believe me? I've seen her do it. Right, four beers, it is, then. (*He crosses* US *to the sideboard*)

William and Mary swivel

Fiona enters from the kitchen R *with a dish, followed by Frank who is carrying plates. They cross* L, US *of the table. Fiona crosses to her place, puts the dish down and takes the plates from Frank*

Fiona Do stop fussing, darling. They're not as hot as all that. I think this has turned out all right. I hope so.
Frank (*crossing and sitting* R *of the table*) Smells a bit off to me.
Fiona (*sighing*) There's eggs and bacon in the pantry. You've no idea, William, the number of times he's actually got up from the dinner-table and gone off to fry himself eggs and things. It really is terribly disheartening. (*She starts to serve the frigadella on to the plates*)

William and Mary swivel

Bob (*crossing* DS *with the beer and pouring it into Mary's glass*) Here we are, Mary. One for you.
Mary No really, Bob, I . . .
Teresa Bob, she doesn't want any.
Bob (*leaning over Mary*) Well, she's having it whether she likes it or not. I can't sit here drinking alone. It's bloody unsociable.
William Now listen, Bob, I don't think you should . . .
Bob Oh shut up. (*He crosses to the window* R)
Teresa You really are a pig, aren't you. A rude drunk pig.

Mary and William rise

Mary I really think we ought to go . . .
Teresa (*rising and pushing William and Mary down and crossing to* US *of her chair*) No, don't go. If anyone's going, it's the pig.
Bob Me?
Teresa Yes, you.

William and Mary swivel

Fiona William, you know it's terrible having a husband with absolutely no palate.
William Oh dear. I'm so sorry.

William and Mary swivel

Bob If I want to stay here, I shall stay here. (*He moves closer to Teresa half menacing*)

William and Mary swivel

Fiona That's why Frank doesn't really enjoy these occasions.
Frank Oh yes, I do. I'm enjoying it very much.
Mary Oh yes. So am I.

William and Mary swivel

Teresa (*picking up the soup ladle*) I'm warning you, Bob.
William (*apprehensively*) Terry, I don't think I should . . .
Teresa Bob . . .
Bob (*moving closer to Teresa*) Go on then, I dare you.

William and Mary swivel

Frank Just a minute. You interrupted my story about Mrs Whatsername. Now then . . . (*He pauses for thought*)

William and Mary swivel. Teresa swings at Bob with the soup ladle. He ducks and catches her wrist. They struggle silently. William and Mary watch horrified. William and Mary swivel

She was put in charge of refreshments for the office Christmas party— and what do you think she gave us? Have a guess.

William and Mary swivel. Bob forces Teresa to drop the ladle. She kicks him. She runs DSC *where he catches her. William and Mary swivel*

Give up? Hot pot! What do you think of that?

William and Mary swivel. Teresa bites Bob and escapes. He yells and chases her round the table. William and Mary swivel

Christmas office party with the guests weaving in and out with steaming bowls of hot pot.

William and Mary swivel

Mary Is anything the matter?
William Bob, I don't think this is really——

Teresa rushes into the kitchen L *pursued by Bob. William and Mary swivel*

Frank The managing director got some all down his shirt front during the tango.

William and Mary swivel. Teresa screams off

Bob (*off*) Bitch!

William and Mary swivel

Frank Well, he turns on this woman Mrs Taylor—Taylor! That's it. Taylor—and he says, now let me get this right, he says——

William and Mary swivel

Teresa (*off*) Damn you.

William and Mary swivel

Frank Well he really lets her have it. And Mrs Taylor, who's had a few herself by then, says—how did she put it now . . .?

William and Mary swivel

Teresa backs on from the kitchen L

Teresa Keep away, Bob—keep away. I'm warning you.
William Bob, for heaven's sake . . .

Bob follows Teresa on from the kitchen L

William and Mary swivel

Frank I know what she said——

William and Mary swivel. Teresa picks up the soup tureen

William Terry!
Mary No!
William (*leaping between Teresa and Bob*) Bob, I—Terry—no!

Teresa throws the soup. It hits William square on. He staggers to his chair, and sits. William and Mary swivel

Frank That's right! Mrs Taylor says——

Teresa rushes out of the front door. Bob follows her laughing

Mrs Taylor says—you're wet!
William (*laughing appreciatively*) Oh! Very good.
Frank No, no. You are wet.
William Oh. Oh, dear, there appears to be a drip.
Frank Drip?
Fiona Darling, you haven't left the shower on again?
Frank Of course not. Anyway, William isn't sitting under the bathroom. He's under the—er—other place.

They all gaze towards the ceiling

CURTAIN

ACT II

SCENE 1

The same. Saturday morning

Set as in Act I, Scene 1 except the two R seats of the sofa now match the Phillips' decor and the L seat matches the Fosters' decor. A sign hangs on the inside of Teresa's front door saying "Goodbye Forever"

Bob, clad only in his trousers, enters from R and crosses to C

Bob (*calling*) Terry! Terry! (*He stares round, sees the sign and slumps in the armchair DL*)

Frank bursts in UL as before. He reaches the timer on table R of the C chair and pulls up short, delighted that it has not rung. He looks at his own watch congratulating himself. He looks at the timer again for confirmation. His smile fades. He clicks it, shakes it, listens to it—finally bangs it. He is very put out. He strides off into the kitchen R

As he does so Bob's doorbell rings. Bob is startled, then smiles rather smugly. He rises and crosses US to the front door UR

(*Flinging the door open*) Home again then, eh? Wouldn't kindly old mother shelter little red riding drawers from the big bad—eh?

Mary is on the doorstep

Mary (*stepping in and stepping back again*) Hallo.
Bob Come in. Do come in.
Mary Thank you. (*She enters and crosses DS of the step*)

Bob slams the door

(*Jumping*) Is er . . . (*She peers round*)
Bob (*crossing close to Mary on her L*) A little chillier this morning, don't you think? Though it might brighten later. Don't like the look of those clouds though, do you. Could have a little rain, don't you agree? Or even snow. You know what they say—red sky in the morning, shepherds warning. Red sky at night your roof is alight. What can I do for you?
Mary I . . .
Bob (*courteously*) Sit down.
Mary (*crossing and sitting on the R end of the sofa*) Thank you.

Bob also re-seats himself DL

Bob Can I—do anything for you?
Mary No. I just wanted a word with Terry, you see.
Bob She's not here.

Mary No. Will she be back?

Bob It's unlikely.

Mary Oh, I see.

Bob All the signs seem to indicate that she's gone for good.

Mary Oh.

Bob She's walked out before, you see, but I've been making a quick inventory and this time she seems to have taken quite a comprehensive collection of essential items with her. One nightie, one toothbrush, at at least two sets of underwear, a long playing record of Benjamin Britten's *War Requiem* and the baby.

Mary But what made her go?

Bob I don't know. She may have eloped with the editor of *The Guardian*.

Mary Who's he?

Bob Yes. Failing that, I repeat, what can I do for you?

Mary It's just—if we could help in any way?

Bob Help?

Mary Well, last night—that soup and things—I just thought that if there was anything that William and I could do to help . . .?

Bob No. That's all cleaned up, thank you.

Mary I didn't mean that.

Bob Didn't you?

Mary I meant—help. You know.

Bob That's very nice of you.

Mary (*warming*) I mean, I thought if you and William were going to be working together, we ought——

Bob We ought to be able to get together. Quite.

Mary Yes.

Bob Where is he?

Mary Mmm?

Bob Why hasn't he come with you?

Mary does not reply

He knows you're here, doesn't he?

Mary Well, I . . .

Bob Oh. He doesn't feel as strongly as you, the urge to help? Is that it?

Mary Well, we talked about it last night—only he felt we shouldn't interfere.

Bob Ah.

Mary This was my idea. William always says I'm too—retiring. That I must get interested, talk to people, you see. Because it's important to talk to people, isn't it? Making social contact is essential. If you're going to have people coming round and drinking sherry and things you must be able to converse with them. And then I thought, well, perhaps the first thing to do is to get to know you and Terry. Perhaps talk over problems. That sort of thing. Just generally sort of help. I mean, that's what we're on this earth for, isn't it?

Bob Good point.

Mary Thank you.

Bob Yes. (*He rises and crosses to* US *of the armchair* C) You're right. Now, there's a broom in the kitchen cupboard and I think you'll find the mop right next to it.

Mary What?

Bob No, I'll tell you what. (*He crosses to* US *of the sofa and leans over the back of the sofa*) Let's not take advantage of friendship. Twenty-five pence an hour, how's that? Thirty-five when you're using the vacuum cleaner because that's pretty heavy. (*He crosses towards the kitchen* L)

Mary (*rising*) I may come back.

Bob Sit down.

Mary No, I really must be——

Bob (*fiercely*) Sit down.

Mary does so. Startled

Mary Don't think you can talk to me the way you talk to Terry.

Bob I wouldn't dream of it. (*He crosses to* R *of the sofa*) Mind you, I'd hate you to go away feeling that I'm ungrateful. I'm not. I'll tell you what, cheer up. (*He sits* R *of Mary*) I'll go and put a shirt on, you go and make us some coffee and then we'll both sit down here and I'll tell you all about our marriage. How would that suit you?

Mary No.

Bob No pleasing you, is there? All right, you tell me about your problems.

Mary I haven't got any problems.

Bob Never mind, we'll soon invent some. (*He pats Mary on the knee, rises and crosses to the kitchen doorway* L) This could be fun.

Mary (*rising*) I ought to go.

Bob Make the coffee—you may even find a cup on the draining board if you dig deep enough.

He exits into the bedroom L

Frank enters with the timer, screwdriver and a coffee from the kitchen R, *crosses to* L *of the double doors, takes a chair and moves it to* US *of the table* L *and sits*

Mary (*sitting*) But I . . .

Frank drops the timer into his coffee and attempts to fish it out with the screwdriver. The doorbell rings

Frank rises and exits UL

Mary rises and crosses towards the front door UR

Bob appears in the bedroom doorway L

He enters and catches Mary creeping towards the front door. He pulls the belt from his trousers, brandishing it threateningly

Bob Hey!

Mary freezes

Coffee, coffee, coffee.

Mary crosses L *and exits into the kitchen* DS *of Bob. Bob exits into the bedroom* L

Frank appears in the hallway UL *with a pram, followed by Teresa*

Frank This is very—unexpected, Terry.
Teresa Yes. I suppose it is. (*She comes into the room* UL *and crosses to* UL *of the sofa*) Sorry.
Frank No, no—a pleasure. A pleasure. Baby'll be all right in the hall, will he? Must say he looks pretty snug and tucked away. (*He leans over the pram*) Oo-hoo!
Teresa Oh, yes, but let him sleep.

Frank enters the room UL *and crosses to* US *of the* C *armchair*

Must have been the bus journey. As soon as we got on he dropped off.
Frank Dropped off?
Teresa To sleep.
Frank Ah. Now, then. Do sit down.
Teresa (*sitting at the* L *end of the sofa*) Thanks.
Frank Can I get you some coffee?
Teresa No, thank you.
Frank (*crossing to* L *of the armchair*) I would offer you mine, but it seems to have a hair-spring in it. Now, what can I do for you? (*He stands a bit awkwardly, wondering why she has come*)

Teresa broods for a moment

Teresa I was on the bus you see . . .
Frank Were you? Yes. Nothing like a bus ride on a Saturday morning—
Teresa I was on my way to my mother's . . .
Frank Ah! Were you? Nice the way you young people communicate with your parents.
Teresa And I thought I must talk to someone. Anyone. Then we passed the end of your road and I thought of you. So I got off.
Frank Glad you did. Glad you did. Still, your mother will be a bit disappointed. I suppose you sent old Bob on ahead, hm?
Teresa I've left him, Frank.
Frank Where?
Teresa We've separated, you see. At least I have.
Frank (*stunned*) Good Lord. (*He crosses and sits in the armchair* C) Good Lord—I don't know what to say—I—Good Lord, good grief. But this is shocking news, Terry. Absolutely shocking.
Teresa I don't know who this other woman is, but . . .
Frank Woman?
Teresa (*muttering*) He's got another woman.
Frank Another one? Must be catching.
Teresa What?
Frank Nothing. You've no idea who she is, I suppose?
Teresa No idea.

Frank Fiona'll be shattered you know.

Teresa Will she?

Frank Oh absolutely. Always been particularly fond of you both.

Teresa So I'm being boringly conventional and running home to mother.

Frank No, no, no. You get on all right with her, do you?

Teresa I shouldn't think so. We'll be at each other's throats in five minutes. I think she prefers Bob, really. I'm too much like my father.

Frank Well, you'll have to talk to him, then.

Teresa He left us in nineteen fifty-three.

Frank Ah. Listen, Terry, are you absolutely certain about this?

Teresa Oh yes. He's been gone nineteen years.

Frank No, I mean, you and Bob. (*He rises and crosses to* L *of the armchair*) You're such a jolly little couple—jolly little flat—jolly little baby. All your future in front of you. (*He crosses to* L *of Teresa*) Oh, I know we all make jokes about Bob being the office Romeo . . .

Teresa Really? I didn't know.

Frank No, no, no. Men's jokes. Nothing serious.

Teresa This is serious.

Frank Yes, of course. Are you quite sure of your facts? Got any concrete evidence?

Teresa Enough. Staying out till all hours in the morning . . .

Frank Yes, well, that isn't really evidence. (*He crosses and sits* C) I mean, take me for instance. I could turn round and say—where on earth is Fiona at the moment. And the answer would be—I haven't the slightest idea. But I certainly don't imagine she's in bed with the chap next door. More probably at the hairdressers.

Teresa Presumably she doesn't stop at the hairdressers till three o'clock in the morning, though.

Frank No, I don't think she does.

Teresa Well, then?

Frank She has been out till that time, though.

Teresa Has she?

Frank Lord, yes. Not frequently, mind you, but occasionally. Why only the other day—when was it—last—wedding anniversary—Wednesday, she was out till all hours.

Teresa Wednesday?

Frank Yes, Wednesday. Really very late.

Teresa Wednesday?

Frank Still you don't want to talk about me—it's your problems we're after.

Teresa Wednesday?

Frank Tell you what I'll do. I'll have a word with old Bob—see if I can get to the bottom of it. He'll have to listen to me.

Teresa Yes!

Frank (*picking up the phone and dialling*) Yes! I'll read him the riot act, shall I?

Teresa Oh! No.

Frank No? Oh, well. (*He replaces the phone*) Second thoughts are very often best. (*He rises*) Look are you sure I can't get you something to drink?

Teresa (*thoughtfully*) No thanks.

Frank Tea? Coffee? (*He crosses to* L *of Teresa*) It's all bubbling away out there.

Teresa Thanks.

Frank You will?

Teresa Yes, please.

Frank crosses DS *of the sofa and turns at the* DR *corner*

Oh, yes!

Frank Yes! Black or white?

Teresa Black, please.

Frank (*going to leave again, then turning*) Coffee?

Teresa Yes, please.

Frank Right.

He exits into the kitchen R

Mary enters from the kitchen L *and crosses* DS *of the sofa with a duster and dustpan. She kneels* D *of the sofa and starts tidying*

Bob enters from the bedroom L *and crosses to* C

Teresa takes out and lights a cigarette

Bob What are you doing?

Mary (*startled*) Oh. Just having a little dust.

Bob Where's the coffee?

Mary You won't get any if you talk like that.

Bob crosses to US *of the sofa and leans over the back watching Mary dust*

Bob Look, would you mind leaving my house alone?

Mary I'm only cleaning up a little.

Bob Well don't. My wife spent a great deal of time and trouble accumulating that dust. And in five minutes you've undone years of her work.

Mary (*moving to* R *of the sofa on her knees*) Don't be silly.

Bob You're a home wrecker. That's what you are.

Mary You don't want a dirty house.

Bob Why not?

Mary Well it's—dirty.

Bob Look. Do me a favour and make the bloody coffee.

Mary rises and crosses to C, *Bob crosses* R *of the sofa*

Mary (*getting angry for her*) You are very, very, very rude. (*She turns and crosses to* US *of the sofa*) I don't know how Terry puts up with you—Oh.

Bob She doesn't any more, does she? (*He laughs*) Coffee, coffee!

Mary exits into the kitchen L, *followed by Bob who exits into the bathroom*

Fiona comes in from the front door UL

Fiona Hallo, Terry. How are you?

Teresa Oh, quite well.

Fiona I wondered what that heaving package in the hall was. It's your baby, isn't it?

Teresa Probably.

Fiona Sweet. (*She crosses and puts the dress box, bag and gloves on the table* L) What a simply dolly pushchair. Beautifully bright and gay.

Teresa It's a carry-cot actually. On wheels.

Fiona Oh, is that what it is? Super. Sweetie, you won't mind my saying so but it does look as if he's drooled just a teeny bit on the carpet.

Teresa Oh. Yes, he often does that.

Fiona Oh, it doesn't matter as long as he's all right. Fearful old carpet anyway, probably brightens it up.

Frank enters from the kitchen R *with a cup*

Frank (*crossing to* UL *of the sofa*) Ah, Fiona. Thank God you're here. I'm afraid you're going to have to brace yourself.

Fiona Why?

Frank Terry's just dropped a bombshell.

Fiona Has she?

Frank Bob's got another woman.

Fiona Another one?

Frank A lover, dear. A love affair.

Fiona Oh. Well—I'm—absolutely amazed.

Frank They've split up, you see.

Fiona Really?

Frank Terry's walked out.

Fiona (*crossing to* L *of the armchair* C) I can't believe you'd do that.

Teresa No. Well I haven't actually.

Frank Haven't? But I thought you said . . .

Teresa I've been thinking it over. You were absolutely right.

Frank Was I? Oh—good.

Teresa After all, why should I give him up? We keep saying it's a love affair but it probably wasn't anything of the sort.

Frank Quite.

Fiona Quite.

Teresa Knowing Bob—it's far more likely to be some rich, old boot he decided to take out for a giggle.

Frank (*amused*) Rich, old boot. Yes . . .

Teresa (*rising to* R *of Frank*) You've been a big help. Thank you, Frank.

Frank Not at all—least I could do.

Teresa Well—I must dash. (*She crosses* US *to the double doors*) Bye then.

Fiona Bye!

Teresa (*to Fiona*) Sorry about the mess—in the hall.

Fiona (*crossing to* L *of the steps*) Perfectly all right.

Teresa You won't mind if I leave you to clean it up, will you?

She blows Fiona a kiss and goes out into the hall, closing the door behind her

Frank Good morning's work. Good morning's work.
Fiona Darling, what's going on?
Frank (*pacing*) Tell you in a second. This needs a little more thought.
Fiona Oh? (*She crosses to the table* L *and opens the dress box*) Darling, I bought that dress by the way.
Frank Right.
Fiona It looks simply ghastly on.
Frank Good.
Fiona But I bought it anyway.
Frank Great.
Fiona I'll tell you what, I'll put it on. You can tell me what you think.
Frank Right.
Fiona Everything all right?
Frank Fine.

Fiona goes out into the hall with an apprehensive look at Frank

Frank comes to a decision, crosses to the phone and starts dialling

Mary enters from the kitchen L *with Bob's coffee*

Mary Here you are then, you don't—oh!—Bob!

There is no reply, then Bob starts singing off, in the bathroom

Bob (*off, singing*) Bless this house, dear Lord, we pray,
        Now my wife has gone away.

Mary, disapproving, puts down the mug and starts dusting. Phillips' phone rings. She looks at it for a moment, uncertainly. She glances off, but there's no sign of Bob. She answers it, uncertainly. She is obviously far from happy using the telephone

Mary Hallo.
Frank Hallo.
Mary Hallo.
Frank Hallo . . . Hallo . . .
Mary Mr Phillips' residence.
Frank Who's that? His maid?
Mary No, it's me.
Frank Who's me?
Mary Mary. Mary Featherstone.
Frank Mary Featherstone?
Mary I think Mr Phillips is in the bathroom at present.
Frank Mary Featherstone?
Mary Who is that talking please?
Frank What are you doing?
Mary When?
Frank Doing there? What are you doing there?
Mary Dusting.
Frank What?
Mary Dusting. Housework and things.

Frank My God . . .
Mary Beg your pardon?
Frank Look, is Bob there?
Mary I think he's just finishing getting dressed.
Frank Great heavens above.
Mary Hallo . . . Could you tell me who's talking please?
Frank What?
Mary Could you tell me your name?
Frank No. Wrong number. Sorry, wrong number.
Mary Can I give him a message at all?
Frank No, no . . .
Mary Who shall I say telephoned?
Frank Er—Mr—er—Mr—er—Mr Carrycot. I'll call back. Goodbye.
  (*He slams down the phone*) Good grief. (*He sits in the armchair* C)

  Bob enters from the bathroom L

Bob (*crossing to* US *of the* C *armchair drying his hands*) Who was that?
Mary (*replacing the receiver she is still holding*) A Mr Carrycot I think he
  said . . .
Bob Oh yes? What did he want?
Mary He said he'd call back. (*She crosses to* US *of the sofa*)
Bob Never heard of him. Perhaps it's my wife's solicitor. Or possibly the
  editor of *The Guardian*.
Mary (*impressed*) Oh.

  Bob exits into bedroom L

  Frank dials. Mary crosses to the table R, *and puts papers into a folder*

Frank Hallo, is that William Featherstone . . . oh, this is Frank Foster
  here . . . yes, good-morning to you . . . hope I haven't caught you in the
  middle of anything . . . You were what? . . . lagging the pipes were
  you? . . . jolly good . . . wish I could say the same . . . Look, listen
  William . . . er . . . Mary isn't there with you, is she? . . . oh . . . no, no
  it doesn't matter . . . you don't happen to know where she is, do you? . . .
  No, I don't want to talk to her, no . . . I just wondered if you knew
  where she was, that's all . . . yes, probably, probably walking somewhere, yes . . .

  Mary picks up the coffee and crosses DS *of the sofa and exits into the
  kitchen* L

  Listen William something's cropped up here—in the kitchen . . . yes . . .
  the sink. You don't happen to know anything about—U-bends do
  you? . . . It's just that we appear to have come up against a blockage . . .

  Fiona enters in her new dress

  Will you? That's very good of you. Sorry to interrupt your—er—
  lagging but I'd be—about ten minutes? . . . Five? Splendid. Bye-bye.
  (*He puts the phone down. He does not notice Fiona*) Disastrous.

Fiona I think that's rather brutal, darling.

Frank Absolutely diastrous.

Fiona What if it were shorter?

Frank At this rate, my whole department is liable to splinter into a dozen pieces. I mean, one's heard of the permissive society, but one doesn't expect to find it running through one's own department. I don't know what's got into them all.

Fiona (*crossing to the doors* UL) I don't know what you're talking about, darling.

Frank All of them. The lot of them. (*He rises and crosses to* L *of Fiona*) You included.

Fiona goes towards the door

My God, you're not going out again, are you?

Fiona I thought I'd take this off as you don't like it.

Frank I have a little matter to discuss with you.

Fiona Really?

Frank Yes. (*He guides Fiona to* R *of the armchair*) Sit down.

Fiona (*slightly apprehensive*) Darling, don't start getting all paternal.

Frank Sit down, please.

Fiona sits in the armchair C

(*Standing to* R *of Fiona*) I think I'm owed an explanation.

Fiona (*rising*) Well, I really do have a lot——

Frank Wednesday night.

Fiona (*sitting*) Wednesday night?

Frank Last Wednesday night.

Fiona Yes?

Frank Where were you?

Fiona I was—I was—well, I—I told you.

Frank You told me you were out with Mary. Mary Featherstone.

Fiona Oh, did I?

Frank Point one. And this I tended to overlook at the time. When the Featherstones were round here on Thursday I mentioned this—so called meeting to Mary. She denied all knowledge of it.

Fiona Did she?

Frank Yes. As I say. I took the matter no further. If for some reason you were doing something on Wednesday night that you didn't want me to know about, fair enough. No business of mine.

Fiona That's—very sporting of you, darling. (*She rises and crosses to the table* L)

Frank However, after Terry left this morning I phoned the Phillips' house, and all is now clear to me. I now understand what it was you were trying to conceal on Wednesday night. And it is a very serious matter.

Fiona (*turning and facing Frank*) I see.

Frank Quite honestly, dear, I'm rather disappointed in you.

Fiona I suppose you must be.

Frank Why you should choose to conspire to conceal this rather sordid business from me, I don't know. Deliberately covering up, and rather badly at that . . .

Fiona I thought—you might be hurt, I suppose.

Frank Well, I am. I am hurt . . . (*He crosses to* L *of Fiona and examines the label on her dress*) You've got a label hanging off you, did you know? I am very hurt.

Fiona Yes, darling.

Frank I mean surely we can share these things, together.

Fiona Share them?

Frank These intimacies?

Fiona Oh, well. It's not usual, surely . . .

Frank I know. You women. Thick as thieves. (*He crosses to the doors* UL) Well, I think I'm going to put some trousers on before William comes.

Fiona (*crossing to the steps* DL *of Frank*) What do you want me to do?

Frank You? You're all right dressed as you are, aren't you?

Fiona No, I mean about us.

Frank Us? Don't quite follow you. Make us a drop more coffee if you like. That'd be a help.

Frank exits UL

Fiona Oh Lord.

Fiona picks up the coffee cups and exits into the kitchen R

Mary enters from the kitchen L *and crosses* DS *with a vacuum cleaner. She carries it to* DR *of the sofa and looks for a plug and finally crawls under the table* DR

Teresa enters UR, *sees the vacuum cleaner gliding across the floor, picks up the tray from the Welsh dresser and crosses* DR *and bangs it on the table*

Teresa I'm back!

Mary pokes her head out from under the table. Teresa crosses and leans against the table US *of Mary*

Oh. Hallo.

Mary Hallo, Terry.

Teresa What are you doing here, for heaven's sake? Have you taken up charring or something?

Mary I thought I might be able to help, you see.

Teresa Help?

Mary I mean after last night—the soup and so on.

Teresa Oh, I see. Well, jolly nice of you. (*She crosses to* C) I shouldn't do any more, this place is a job for life. (*She crosses* US, L *of the armchair* C *and sees papers on the table and crosses* R, *to* US *of the table* R) Hell's bloody bells, who's been at this lot?

Mary Oh. (*She comes out from under the table and rises to* L *of Teresa*) I think I just straightened——

Teresa Oh, no. They're in a fine old muck now.

Mary I'm sorry, have I . . .?

Teresa It's just I had them all sorted out, you see, love. They're all my press cuttings. All the articles I clip out from papers. I had birth control, famine relief and chemical warfare all in separate piles. Now they're all in a bloody jumble.

Fiona enters from the kitchen R crosses to the phone and dials

Mary I'm terribly sorry . . .

Teresa Oh Lord, all my letters are in here, too.

Mary Letters?

Teresa Copies of the ones I send to the editor of *The Guardian*—that's all.

Teresa's phone rings

Mary Oh.

Teresa answers the phone. Mary crosses to her R

Teresa Hallo.

Fiona gives a huge sigh of annoyance

(*Infuriated*) Pervert!

Fiona drops the phone and exits rapidly into the kitchen R

Teresa slams the phone down and crosses back to the table R. Mary backs away L

Bob enters from the kitchen L and stands in the doorway

Mary and Teresa look at him

Bob Well, well, well.

Teresa Hallo. (*She crosses to the UR corner of the sofa*)

Teresa and Bob face each other. Mary stands, fascinated

Bob Forget something, did you?

Teresa No.

Bob Oh. Thought you might have popped back for alimony.

Teresa (*studying him. After a pause*) You know, deep down inside, you're really rotten, aren't you?

Bob You should know.

Teresa God. I know.

Bob Where's Benjie?

Teresa Asleep.

Bob Oh. Come here, then.

Teresa Oh no.

Bob Come here.

Teresa No. (*She pauses*) You come here.

Mary, who knows she ought to leave, can't. She's riveted

Bob All right. (*He moves to Teresa*)

Mary retreats a pace, nervously, expecting violence. Bob reaches Teresa and faces her. His hand goes slowly to the back of her head and he takes her hair. Mary crosses to L of Bob

(*Gently*) Silly cow.
Teresa (*the same*) Bastard.

Bob and Teresa embrace

Fiona's doorbell rings

Fiona enters from the kitchen R and crosses and exits UL

Teresa crosses DS of Bob, takes his hand and draws him across L, DS of Mary to the kitchen doorway L

(*Turning just before they exit*) Try not to wake Benjamin, love, won't you.

Bob and Teresa exit into the bedroom L

Mary crosses and leans on the table R

William enters UL brandishing a monkey wrench and crosses DS. Fiona follows to his R

William Came round as quickly as I could. (*He waves the wrench*) This will do the trick.
Fiona Oh?
William Have you fixed up in no time.
Fiona Good. Thank you. (*She pauses*) My husband won't be a moment.
William Ah. Coping with the emergency, is he?
Fiona Well, he's just putting on some trousers.
William Oh, I see. I hope I haven't called at an inconvenient time?
Fiona No, not at all. Do sit down.

William sits in the armchair C. Fiona crosses to DS of the sofa

Mary picks up the vacuum cleaner and exits into the kitchen L

William May I take this opportunity of thanking you on behalf of my wife and myself for a delightful meal the other evening.
Fiona Thank you.
William Thank you.

A pause. Fiona smiles awkwardly at William. He smiles back

That's a very attractive dress, if I may say so.
Fiona Oh. Do you think so. Thank you.
William And brand new on today, unless I'm very much mistaken.
Fiona Yes?
William Yes. I've spotted your little label.
Fiona Oh that, yes.
William Overlooked that, hadn't you?
Fiona No, actually, I left it on deliberately.
William Oh?

Fiona I've tried it without, but I've come to the conclusion that I prefer the dress with the label on.

William Oh. I'm sorry, in that case.

Fiona Quite all right. (*She sits at the* L *end of the sofa*) I wonder if you could tell me something.

William I'll have a go.

Fiona I want to ask you a theoretical question. It's purely theoretical, mark you. I just want to know how you think you'd react.

William All right. Fire ahead.

Fiona If you—er . . . If you found out that your wife was having an affair with another man, how would you react?

William What an extraordinary question.

Fiona Yes, it is rather, isn't it?

William I mean, Mary would never dream of it.

Fiona Of course not, I did say it's theoretical.

William I see. (*He considers*) Well . . .

Fiona I mean, do you for instance think you'd say—I'm rather disappointed in you. You might have shared it with me. Something like that?

William No. I don't think I'd say that. Hit her—perhaps? Sorry I can't be more help. I've had no real experience of that sort of situation.

Fiona Nor have I.

Frank enters UL

He crosses to L *of William and claps his hands expectantly. William rises*

Frank Ah.

Fiona starts nervously

Sorry. Hallo there, William. Nice of you to drop round.

William I was just saying—I came as soon as I could.

Frank I'm glad you did. Now the first thing is we must all have a drink and—(*he pushes William down and crosses* US *to the drinks cabinet*)— then we must sit down and have a talk.

Fiona crosses to L *of Frank. Frank hands her a sherry*

Fiona Yes, well I'll just pop upstairs, darling, and——

Frank No, no, no. Need you here with us. Sit down.

Fiona Well, I really——

Frank Sit down. (*He guides Fiona back to the sofa*)

Fiona sits with her sherry

(*Crossing to the drinks cabinet and picking up a sherry*) You've got to have a drink. We've all got to have a drink.

William Well, it's a bit early, but still . . .

Frank I absolutely insist. (*He crosses to* R *of William and hands him a sherry*) Here we are then.

William Thank you very much.

Frank The toast is "Steady the Buffs".

Fiona Steady the Buffs?

Frank Now then. Let's get down to it. William——

William Er—the . . .

Frank What's that?

William U-bend?

Frank Do I?

William No, the one I've come over to look at.

Frank Oh, that U-bend. Yes. Well, that's the first thing, William.

William What is?

Frank (*taking the monkey wrench from William*) There is no U-bend.

William But I thought . . .

Frank I'm afraid you thought wrongly. The U-bend was merely an excuse to get you over here.

William Why?

Fiona Darling, what is going on?

Frank (*crossing to* L *of William and putting the monkey wrench on the table* L) If you will allow me to, I will explain. I'm afraid, William, that what I have to say will come as rather a shock. I'm sorry to say that my wife has been deceiving me—that's why I have asked her to stay here so that she can tell you about the whole sordid business from start to finish.

Fiona You can't be serious!

Frank Hmm?

Fiona You expect me calmly to sit here, and tell—William everything? (*She rises to* R *of William*) Is that what you're getting at?

Frank That's the general idea, yes.

Fiona And just what are you trying to do—humiliate me?

Frank No, dear. William has the right to know.

Fiona William has the right to know? Oh, well then, in that case, invite the postman in. Invite the butcher—if you really want to humiliate me, why not make a real show of it?

Frank What's the postman got to do with it?

Fiona I think this is really sinking very low. I mean, at least if you hit me that would show you cared. Go on! Hit me! Hit me!

Frank Have you had a bit of a bang already this morning? Got a bit overheated under the hairdryer or something?

Fiona (*leaning over William*) Don't try to be funny with me!

William Pardon, I'm not quite sure . . .

Fiona The point is, William, that my husband is trying to tell you, in a rather sordid way, about a very silly, very trivial love affair between Bob Phillips and . . . (*She turns away from William*)

Frank And your wife, William. Precisely. I think you could have put it a bit better than that. I was trying to spare the poor chap's feelings.

William My wife? (*He rises*)

Frank (*pushing William down and patting him on the shoulder*) Sorry, old chap. You had to know sooner or later.

Fiona His wife? You mean Mary Featherstone?

Frank Of course I mean Mary Featherstone. Only got one wife, hasn't he? I hope.

William My wife and Bob Phillips?

Fiona Darling, you can't mean it? Bob Phillips and Mary Featherstone?

Frank Mary Featherstone and Bob Phillips. I wish everyone wouldn't keep repeating the damn thing.

Fiona (*crossing and sitting at the L end of the sofa*) That's utterly ridiculous.

William I've never heard anything so—absurd . . .

Frank Yes, I know, it must be an absolute wallop in the old bread-basket for you, William, but there it is. (*He crosses to L of Fiona*) I don't know why you're sounding so surprised all of a sudden, darling. You've been covering up for the wretched girl for three days.

Fiona Covering up?

William Absolutely absurd . . .

Frank (*turning to William*) Now let's be totally fair about this, William. You haven't been exactly guiltless yourself, have you? Now, there's not much escapes me, so don't try and deny it. I quite appreciate this is hardly the moment to remind you of your own sorties with those boots of yours and so on.

William Boots?

Frank The ones you keep on top of the filing cabinet. I know all about those, too, you see.

William Those are my potholing boots.

Frank No, I'm not really interested in what name you choose to call it, William. I just want to deal, perfectly calmly with the facts. Last Wednesday night my wife returned home very late indeed and informed me that she had been spending an evening with Mary. This, I have since discovered, was palpably untrue.

Fiona Darling, you have got hold of the most——

Frank Sssh, please! May I just . . .? This story was an invention of my wife's . . .

William Was it, Mrs Foster?

Fiona Well, in a way, yes. But I——

Frank You see.

Fiona But I certainly wasn't covering up for Mary.

Frank What other possible reason could you have had for concocting this story? Answer me that?

Fiona (*stumped*) Well—er—no—none at all.

Frank Precisely. I'm afraid that's definitely minus score as far as I'm concerned, darling. (*He crosses to the chair US of the table L*)

William But I can't see that that proves——

Frank (*picking up chair, crossing to L of William, putting down the chair and sitting*) I am coming to that, William. This morning, I had Teresa Phillips round here. She informed me she had discovered her husband to be having an affair. After she left, I phoned Bob Phillips. I spoke to your wife, William. She was in his house——

William At Bob Phillips! What was she doing at Bob Phillips!

Frank I'm trying to spell this out in words of one syllable, William. She answered the phone, pretending, as far as I could judge to be the maid or something. Phillips she informed me was upstairs in the bath. She claimed to be dusting. You can put what interpretation you like on that. To me it only pointed to one thing.

William (*dazed, incredulous*) I—can't believe this—my wife—? Is this true, Mrs Foster?

Fiona I—um-mmmm.

William Of course. That's what you were trying to tell me before your husband came in, wasn't it? How would you react, you said, if you found your wife had been unfaithful to you? And I said——

Fiona You'd hit her—yes, I remember.

William Yes. Did I say that? Yes, that's right. (*He swallows the sherry and rises*)

Frank (*rising*) Now steady, old lad.

William Could I possibly have a drink, please?

Frank Yes, of course, of course. What would you like? Bloody Mary? No—no—scotch? (*He crosses to the drinks cabinet and pours a scotch*) Right.

William crosses to the table and picks up the monkey wrench and crosses to C. *Fiona leaps up and crosses to* R *of William*

Fiona (*taking the monkey wrench*) William, I really would think before you do anything.

Frank crosses to L *of William with his drink*

William Do you realize, Mrs Foster, the hours I've put into that woman? When I met her, you know, she was nothing. Nothing at all. With my own hands I have built her up. Encouraging her to join the public library and make use of her non-fiction tickets—I introduced her to the Concert Classics Record Club—I've coaxed her, encouraged her to think—even perhaps bullied her, some might say. (*He takes the drink from Frank*) Thank you very much. Her dress sense was terrible, my own mother encouraged her towards adventurous cooking—everything. I've done everything.

Fiona Jolly good. Cheers.

William swigs the glass

Frank Hoy. Steady on.

William And then a man like Phillips—Phillips can come along and . . . (*He crosses towards the double doors*) How dare he? How dare he? (*He crosses and bangs glass down on the table*)

Frank Might be a good idea if you stayed for lunch, William.

William How dare he. (*He crosses to the double doors*)

Fiona William, dear, do sit down.

William crosses to Fiona, snatches monkey wrench and crosses US

William How dare he.

   He rushes out UL

Fiona Stop him!

Frank Too late.

Fiona Now look what you've done.

Frank Me?

Fiona You realize that man is in a totally unbalanced state. The mood he's in at the moment, he could shoot someone.

Frank With a monkey wrench? Do you think that's possible? (*He crosses to the phone and starts to dial*) I think I'd better call Bob Phillips and warn him.

Fiona (*crossing* DS, *picking up the chair* L *of the armchair and placing it* L *of the double doors*) They were perfectly happy until you started on them.

Frank Me?

Fiona Yes.

Frank Now look here, I don't think you can really keep on blaming me for this.

Fiona I'm going to change. (*She crosses to the doors* UL) I'm going to get out of this monstrosity.

The Phillips' phone rings

> *Fiona exits* UL

> *Mary enters from the kitchen* L *and crosses to the front door* UR

Frank crosses DS *of the armchair with the phone. Mary crosses and answers the phone*

Mary Hallo.

Frank Hallo.

Mary Hallo. Oh hallo, that's Mr Carrycot, isn't it?

Frank No. Is that you Mary, now——

Mary I'm sorry, Mr Carrycot, Mr Phillips is in the bedroom at the moment.

Frank Mary——

Mary His wife is with him, so I didn't like to disturb them——

Frank Mary listen to me. This is Foster, do you hear? Foster . . .

Mary Who?

Frank Frank Foster.

Mary Oh, I thought you were Mr——

Frank Yes, yes quite. But I'm not. I'm me. Now listen, Mary. This is urgent. You must replace that receiver and leave that house immediately, do you understand?

Mary Yes. But——

Frank Don't argue. Just do as you're told. But before you leave you must go upstairs and tell Phillips to lock himself in that bedroom and stay there.

Mary But I can't go in, he's with his wife.

Frank This is a matter of life and death, woman. Now, Mary, when you've done that. Leave the house. But on no account go to your home. Come straight round here. And run, run, all the way, do you hear? It's vital you do this.

Mary But Mr Foster, I've to get William's dinner. He gets very cross——

Frank William is more than cross just at the moment, Mary, he's——

William bursts through the front door UR

William Mary!

Mary (*looking off to the door*) Oh, talk of the devil, Mr Foster. Here he is.

Frank Take cover! Take cover! (*He kneels* DS *of the armchair* C) Get down on the floor . . .

Mary Beg your pardon?

William Mary! (*He crosses to* US *of the sofa*)

Mary Hallo, William. (*Into the reciver*) Just hold on a minute Mr Foster, will you?

Frank Mary, Mary—for goodness sake . . . (*He realizes he is talking to no-one*) Oh . . . (*He stands holding the receiver anxiously*)

William (*crossing to* R *of Mary*) So, it's true, Mary. It's true.

Mary What?

William I would not have believed this of you, Mary. I would never have believed it. How could you do this? (*He brandishes the monkey wrench and crosses to the table* R *and slams the monkey wrench down. Loudly*) How could you do this?

Mary You're not cross that I came round, are you William?

Frank Mary, can you get hold of a blunt instrument?

William (*turning*) Leave this house! Leave this house, this instant.

Mary But I'm on the telephone . . . (*She starts gnawing her nails*)

William I am warning you, Mary. I am very near to violence. (*He crosses to* R *of Mary and smacks her hand ineffectively*) I have never struck or molested you since the day we were married. Even under these circumstances I do not wish to start. But I shall do so, Mary, I shall do so—If you do not leave this house.

Mary I came round because Terry needed help that's all.

William Terry? Is Terry here, too?

Mary She's in the bedroom with Bob.

William And what sort of help do you intend giving her in there may I ask?

Mary No. She's having a love affair.

William Who is?

Mary Terry. With a man from the newspaper.

Frank My God, another one.

Mary (*into the phone*) Just a minute, Mr Foster . . .

Frank Mary . . .

Mary She writes to him, you see. Bob told me. His name's Mr Carrycot. He's the editor of *The Guardian* . . .

William What a feeble, shabby tale. (*He advances on her*) You deceitful slut!

Frank Hallo!

Bob, in his dressing-gown, enters from the bedroom L *and crosses to* US *of the sofa*

William crosses to R *of Bob*

Bob Look, I'd be grateful if you two would take your domestic quarrels elsewhere.

William leaps forward and swings a blow at Bob. It goes low and catches him in the stomach

William You swine, Phillips. You swine.
Bob (*collapsing on his knees with a grunt*) Aagh!
William That'll teach you!
Mary William!
William (*crossing to* R *of the sofa nursing his hand*) That'll teach you!
Frank Hallo! Hallo!

Fiona enters UL

Fiona Hallo. (*She crosses to* L *of Frank*)
Frank Get down on the floor, dear.
Fiona (*kneeling* L *of Frank*) Darling, what's the matter?
Frank Something going on. No shots yet, thank God, but . . .
William If you get up, I shall hit you again, Phillips. I warn you.
Bob (*rising*) What the hell was that in aid of?
Mary William, are you all right?
Fiona Darling, are you all right?
William I'm all right.
Frank I'm all right.
William I'm the only one in this house that is all right . . .
Bob (*crossing to* R *of the sofa*) What's he on about, Mary? Gone off his rocker has he?

Teresa enters in a housecoat from L

William springs forward again and hits Bob in the eye this time. Bob collapses backwards on to the sofa. Mary, still holding the phone, screams. Frank, who gets this down the phone, yells and jumps back. Fiona, reacting to this, cries out. William's impetus from the blow he has landed Bob sends him, doubled up, past Bob and almost careering into Teresa. She, with a swift, two-handed blow on the back of his neck, floors William completely

Mary drops the phone and exits screaming UR

Teresa tends to Bob

Almost immediately Mary enters UL *through Frank's front door, still screaming*

Frank, who is still shouting advice to Mary down the phone, and Fiona rise in amazement. Mary crosses to stand between Frank and Fiona

Mary I—I—I—aaaah. (*She falls in a dead faint*)

CURTAIN

Scene 2

The same. Sunday morning

Set as in Act I, Scene 1 except all three seats of the sofa now match the Fosters' decor

Frank paces up and down c

Frank Fellow workers—members of my department—let's put our cards on the table . . .

Fiona enters from the kitchen r *with two cups of coffee*

Fiona Coffee?
Frank Just one cup . . .

Fiona gives Frank the coffee

Oh, thank you.
Fiona (*crossing and sitting in the armchair* c) Are you sure this is the right thing?
Frank Absolutely.
Fiona But it really has nothing to do with us.
Frank They're all members of my department. As such I feel their physical and, to a certain extent, spiritual welfare are my concern.
Fiona Oh, darling, that's dreadfully pompous.
Frank There is nothing pompous about human concern. I wonder if you'd mind not sitting there.

Fiona rises and crosses and sits c *of the sofa*

(*Sitting in the armchair* c) Thank you. Where's Mary?
Fiona I've only just woken her. She had a nice long sleep. The best thing for her.
Frank As long as she's down for the meeting.
Fiona She'll be down. Probably starving as well. She ate nothing last night. Not a bite.

The doorbell rings

Frank That'll be the Phillips.

Frank and Fiona rise

Fiona (*crossing* us *to the double doors*) I'll let them in. This isn't going to take too long, I trust. I've put newspaper down in the hall, so their baby can spill anything it likes.

Fiona goes out

Frank paces about

Frank (*muttering*) Team mates—a team that plays together stays together, but some of us have been playing too hard . . . (*He crosses to* UL *of the sofa*) I expect some of you are wondering why I . . .

Teresa, Fiona and Bob enter UL

Fiona Here we are.
Frank (*shaking all three of them by the hand*) Come in. Come in. Come in.
Teresa Hallo, Frank.
Bob Hi, Frank.
Frank Do sit down. Sit down. Sit down.

Teresa crosses and sits at the L *end sofa. Bob crosses and sits in the armchair* C

(*Crossing to* R *of the armchair*) Now, I've asked you here——
Fiona (*calling*) Mary!
Bob What's it all about?
Frank Well, I've asked you——
Fiona (*crossing to the kitchen* R) I'll bring you some coffee.

She goes out

Frank I've asked . . . (*He notices Bob's bruised face*) That's a nasty knock, Bob. Where'd you get that?
Bob That's an interesting story, actually.
Teresa William did it.
Frank William? I see.
Bob More than we do.
Frank Exactly. I wonder if you'd mind not sitting . . .

Bob rises and crosses and sits C *of the sofa*

(*Crossing* DS *of the armchair*) Thank you. Now, the idea of this morning is to try and undo some of the damage.

Fiona enters from the kitchen R *with a coffee tray and puts it down on the table* L

Fiona Coffee? Bob? Terry?
Bob Thanks.
Teresa Thank you.

Fiona pours the coffee

Frank The point is, Terry——
Fiona Terry, white?
Teresa Please.
Frank Terry——
Fiona Sugar?
Teresa Two, please.

Fiona hands Teresa her coffee

Frank Terry! Let's keep calm, shall we? I did warn you on the phone that we may be in for some nasty shocks——
Fiona You're both looking terribly well.
Teresa Are we?
Fiona I love your bruise, Bob. How did you get it?

Bob Oh, I—picked it up fairly cheaply somewhere.

Fiona (*handing Bob his coffee*) Suits you. I should keep it. (*She crosses to* US *of the sofa*)

Frank I really must insist that we keep to the subject. We have a lot to get through this morning.

Bob This has the air of a rather seedy annual general meeting. Where exactly do Terry and I come into it?

Frank That's a pretty cynical thing to say, Bob. Considering.

Teresa Oh, what have you been doing now?

Bob Me?

Teresa Yes.

Bob Nothing.

Frank Will you please address your remarks through the chair. Now, Bob, before Mary comes down, and before William gets here——

Bob (*jumping up*) William!

Frank Oh, do sit down, Bob.

Bob I'm not staying here. That man's unbalanced.

Frank I wouldn't go so far as to say unbalanced.

Fiona crosses to US *of the armchair* C *and perches on the back of the chair*

I agree it was a rather drastic course of action to take, but understandable, under the circumstances.

Bob Oh, perfectly understandable. He's off his nut, that's all. (*He sits*)

Frank Darling, would you mind not . . .?

Fiona crosses to US *of the sofa*

Now before Mary comes down, and before——

Mary enters UL *on to the steps*

Fiona (*crossing up to the steps*) Ah. Here she is.

Mary crosses to L *of the armchair* C

(*Crossing to* US *of the sofa*) Mary, come in and sit down.

Mary Hallo.

Teresa Hallo, Mary.

Mary sits in the armchair C

Frank No, not there, Mary, please!

Mary leaps up and crosses to the sofa. Bob moves to the R *end and Mary sits* C

Fiona Coffee, Mary?

Mary Thank you.

Fiona pours the coffee

Frank I was just saying, Mary, that the reason we're all here is that we want to try and put things right for you.

Fiona (*handing Mary her coffee*) Mary.

Mary Thank you.
Frank Not at all. The point is, that when William arrives——
Mary (*jumping up*) William! Oh no.
Frank Oh, do sit down, Mary.

Mary sits

You're quite safe.
Mary I don't think I can——
Frank When William arrives, you must be quite straight and honest with
   him. Don't try and pretend it's anything less than it is—a love affair—
   a perfectly ordinary love affair between yourself and Bob Phillips.
Mary A what?
Bob Eh?
Teresa What?
Frank (*a bit startled by their reaction crossing* DS) Well, those are the
   facts, aren't they?
Bob Frank. You must be joking.
Frank Hardly a subject for—mirth, I'd have thought.
Mary I haven't had an affair with Bob—honestly, Terry.
Teresa (*laughing*) No, I do believe you.
Frank Well, in that case I—are you sure you haven't?
Bob Where the hell did you get that idea?
Frank Um. Well, it came in dribs and drabs, really.
Bob I see.
Frank Oh, well, if you haven't had an affair, we'll have to change the
   agenda. (*He crosses* DL) It certainly makes things a lot simpler.

The doorbell rings. Mary jumps up. Teresa pulls her down

Mary William!
Fiona Oh Lord.

   Fiona goes out UL *to answer the door*

Bob Is that why he hit me?
Frank Presumably.
Bob It's always nice to know—when one is struck down in one's own
   sitting-room.
Teresa You'd be a fat lot of good in a crisis. You didn't even put up
   a fight.
Bob I didn't know there was a fight.

   William enters UL *and crosses to* R *of Frank. Fiona enters* UL *and crosses
   to* UL *of the sofa*

William I came as quickly as I could. I don't know much about immersion
   heaters but I'll see what . . . Oh. (*He glares at the assembled company*)
Frank Ah, William.
Bob Hallo.
William Is this some sort of humorous prank?
Frank William——

William Not very amusing at all. Inviting me here and then confronting me with him and her. Do you think I want to sit down in the same room as them?

Frank William——

William I still have a blinding headache, and I have been up half the night with one. I came round here in good faith to have a look at the thermostat on your immersion heater—as you requested . . .

Frank William!

William (*startled*) Uh? Yes?

Frank There's been a misunderstanding, William.

Bob You could call it that.

Frank The point is—er—I think I misinformed you.

William What about?

Bob About Mary and me.

Frank My information was inaccurate. (*He crosses to* UL *of the armchair* C)

William You mean . . .?

Bob shakes his head, then Mary shakes her head

    I see.

Fiona (*crossing to* C) I suggest, William, the very best thing you can do is to take Mary home and have a lovely lunch together and then you can both kiss and make up—I'll see you all out. (*She crosses* US *to the double doors*)

Bob and Teresa rise. Teresa crosses to DL *of the steps and Bob crosses to the* UL *corner of the sofa*

William (*crossing to* D) *of the armchair*) Well, I don't quite know what to say. I've been badly misled.

Bob (*crossing to* R *of William*) You should have checked your facts first, shouldn't you?

William Well—I'm sorry, Bob. I—er—I hope you weren't too badly hurt?

Bob Not too badly, at all. Short spell in the iron lung and I'll be fine.

Teresa (*crossing to* L *of William*) How's your head?

William Not so bad, I——

Teresa Sorry about that, too.

William No, no. My fault entirely.

Bob and Teresa cross to the steps

    Well, I think the best thing is for us both to leave now—rather than——

Fiona You haven't had coffee?

William No, no thank you, Mrs Foster.

Fiona crosses to R *of the steps*

    Mary?

Mary Yes?

William Come along. (*He crosses to the steps, between Bob and Teresa*)

Mary Just a minute.

William, Teresa, Bob and Fiona turn to Mary

William Yes?

Mary What about me? You've apologized to everyone else, what about me?

William I don't have to apologize to you. I was misled.

Mary How?

William (*crossing to* UL *of the sofa*) Surely you've grasped the situation. I was told——

Mary You've always told me, never believe everything people tell you.

William True, but——

Mary Then why did you?

William That's an entirely different—Mr Foster told me——

Mary I want an apology.

Fiona, Bob and Teresa cross DS

William (*crossing to* L *of the sofa*) Mary, don't start a scene here.

Mary I'm not leaving here till I get an apology.

William Darling, I shall get angry.

Bob (*crossing to* US *of the sofa*) Go on—apologize.

William Do you mind?

Teresa crosses to UL *of the armchair. Fiona crosses to* UL *of the sofa*

Teresa I think you owe her an apology, William.

William Thank you very much, Terry, I'll deal with my own affairs.

Frank I'd apologize if I were you, old chap. Much the easiest thing to do.

William Oh. Well—if you say so, Mr Foster.

Frank Decent thing to do.

William In that case I'm—I'm—I'm . . . (*He can't say it*)

Mary That'll do. (*She rises and crosses* L *and shakes Frank's hand, crosses* UR *and shakes Fiona's hand and crosses into doorway* UL) Thank you. We'll go now. Thank you very much, Mr Foster, Mrs Foster for looking after me.

Fiona A pleasure.

Frank Goodbye, Mary. Best of luck.

Mary Thank you. William?

William steps forward. He continues spluttering and gesticulating for some moments but is unable to do anything. Finally:

William Cheerio.

William stalks out UL

Mary turns after him and turns back

Mary (*in a low voice, indicating the departed William*) It's difficult for him. He's never been wrong before, you see.

Mary exits UL. *Fiona follows her*

Teresa crosses and shakes Frank's hand

Fiona reappears in the doorway

Fiona Oh, Terry, your baby appears to be eating all that newspaper I put
down for him, in the hall. Is it good for him?
Teresa Depends which one.

Teresa exits UL. *Fiona follows her*

Bob crosses L *and Frank crosses* R. *They meet and shake hands* DS *at the
steps*

Frank Er—just one word of warning, Bob.
Bob What?
Frank Well, when Mary was here last night, couldn't get much out of her,
but she did say something, I think you ought to know. Apparently,
Terry might be getting herself involved with some—newspaper man.
Bob Newspaper man?
Frank Yes, apparently.
Bob You mean one of those blokes who stand on corners shouting.
Frank No, no. Journalist chap.
Bob Oh. Really? Thanks.
Frank Just watch out.
Bob (*puzzled*) Yes, right. Cheerio then.

Bob exits UL

Frank crosses and sits at the end of the sofa

Frank (*rubbing his hands together, pleased*) Good, good, good.

Fiona enters UL

Fiona (*crossing to the table* L *and beginning to stack the cups*) Well done,
darling.
Frank A good morning's work, I think. Good morning's work.
Fiona (*collecting the cups from the coffee-table and taking them to the table*
L) That really is the most awful baby they have. Quite apart from look-
ing like an unsuccessful Hogarth, it's left a large damp patch on our
carpet again. Have to leave the front door open—let it dry out.
Frank (*thoughtful suddenly*) Just a minute. There's something missing.
There's a loose end somewhere . . .
Fiona (*crossing to* L *of Frank and taking his cup*) Yes, well, don't you worry
about that now. You spend much too much time worrying about other
people's problems. (*She crosses to the table* L)
Frank You told me, first, that you were out with Mary on Wednesday last.
Fiona Did I?
Frank Yes. Then you said, under pressure—"No, I was just covering up
for Mary", didn't you?
Fiona Yes, possibly.
Frank However, since Mary was not having an affair, you wouldn't have
needed to cover up for her, would you?

Fiona I suppose not.

Frank No. You wouldn't. So the question remains: what on earth were you up to on Wednesday night?

Fiona Oh, I was—pottering about, you know.

Frank Been behaving rather peculiarly lately, altogether.

Fiona Really?

Frank Yes.

Fiona Good. (*She picks up the tray and turns towards the kitchen*) More coffee?

Frank Where were you?

Fiona (*laughing*) You don't really want to know—do you?

Frank Yes, I do.

Fiona Oh. (*She pauses. She puts tray down and crosses to* L *of the sofa*) Well. Well, I did something rather—silly.

Frank Did you?

Fiona Yes. (*She pauses*) Are you going to be awfully cross with me?

Frank No.

Fiona Well, we sort of met and then we——

Frank Another chap.

Fiona Yes.

Frank Oh.

Fiona It really wasn't anything.

Frank No. Do I know him?

Fiona Sort of.

Frank I see.

Fiona It really wasn't—I mean—nothing—He wasn't half as nice as you.

Frank Oh.

Fiona (*kneeling* L *of Frank and putting arms round his neck*) Are you going to forgive me?

Frank Yes, of course. I mean, nothing much else I can do, is there? So long as you don't make a sort of habit of it.

Fiona (*kissing him on forehead*) Darling.

Frank Hmmmm.

Fiona I'll tell you what. I'll make us a special un-anniversary dinner to make up for it. Something nice. And you can open a bottle of wine and we'll have a squiffy evening together. What about that?

Frank Um?

Fiona I know, I'll put on some of that delicious perfume you bought me after lunch, shall I?

Frank Oh, yes. Do that!

Fiona (*rising, crossing to the table* L, *picking up the tray and crossing towards the kitchen* R) Good.

Frank Fiona? Who was it?

Fiona Who?

Frank This man you . . .?

Fiona Oh. No-one of the least importance.

Frank Someone we know, though?

Fiona It really doesn't matter.

She exits into the kitchen R

Frank (*muttering*) Someone we know . . .? (*He rises, takes the phone-pad from the small table by the armchair* C *and crosses and sits at the* L *end of the sofa. He thumbs through the phone-pad*)

Bob enters UR *and exits into the kitchen* L

Adams—no, Atkinson—Aubrey S—who's Aubrey S? Oh him—no—Associated Dairies—no—(*He continues to mutter*)

Teresa enters UR *and crosses* DS

Bob enters from the kitchen L, *crosses to Teresa and hands her a cigarette*

Teresa What a waste of a morning.

Bob crosses and sits in armchair DL. *Teresa crosses to his* R

Bob I'm sure Frank enjoyed it.
Teresa (*laughing*) You and Mary Featherstone—I'd love to have seen that.
Bob I don't know how the hell Frank got hold of that idea.

They laugh

Teresa Well. Now if he'd said you and Fiona?

Bob stops laughing

Is it over between you two?
Bob What?
Teresa It was pretty obvious.
Bob Oh.

Pause

Teresa Well, if it had to be someone, I'd sooner her than Mary.
Bob So would I.
Teresa No, I mean, Mary's a sticker. If she took a fancy to you, she'd hang on. Fiona knows which side her bread is buttered.

She goes out into the kitchen L

Frank Yates—Yeoman—YMCA . . .

Teresa enters from the kitchen L *and crosses to* R *of Bob with the perfume*

Bob What's that?
Teresa Bottle of perfume. I noticed it on the hall-table at Fiona's. Benjie must have reached out of his carry-cot and taken it.
Bob Oh, yes?
Teresa Quite nice. I think I'll keep it. I think she owes it to me. (*She crosses to the table* R *and sits at the* US *end*) I can't think what you saw in her—apart from promotion.
Bob Come on. What about you?
Teresa Me?

Bob Your friend. The journalist.

Teresa Journalist?

Bob I've heard.

Teresa I don't know any journalists.

Bob No?

Teresa No. I wish I did. You know, you were a fool to do it. Frank's bound to find out sooner or later.

Frank Someone we—ah! Good Lord! Good Lord, yes! Of course. (*He stands for a moment staring at the door as the realization dawns, then goes to the phone and dials*)

Bob rises and crosses towards the kitchen L

Teresa Where are you going?

Bob (*dignified*) I'm going to get the lunch.

Teresa You're what?

Bob I'm going to get the bloody lunch. What's wrong with that?

Bob goes into the kitchen L

Teresa My God!

After a long pause, Teresa's phone rings. Frank is growling menacingly into the phone. Teresa advances, warily, and picks up the phone, and hears Frank growling

That's screwdriver, isn't it?

Frank Screwdriver?

Teresa Oh, good, you're talking. That's a great step forward. Now listen to me. Does it give you some sort of kick phoning up women and trying to frighten them? Does it?

Frank Er—no—not really. I don't think so. I don't really know.

Teresa Look. You obviously need help. Haven't you anyone you can talk to—a wife or a mother?

Frank Mummy's passed away.

Bob enters from the kitchen L *wearing an apron*

Bob (*crossing to Teresa*) Where the hell are all the saucepans?

Teresa (*to Bob*) Sssh!

Fiona enters from the kitchen R *and crosses to Frank*

Frank (*as Fiona enters, misinterpreting, whispers*) And my wife's in the kitchen . . .

Fiona What's that?

Frank (*to Fiona*) Sssh!

Teresa Look, I'm sorry to sound technical, but—are you—very frustrated?

Bob Eh?

Teresa Sssh!

Frank Frustrated?

Teresa You know. Sexually.

Frank Sexually?

Fiona Sexually?!
Frank Sssh!
Teresa Look. I can't talk any more now, but if you want to—ring me up again and we can even meet somewhere and have a session.
Frank Meet somewhere—yes—that'd be nice.
Teresa Good. Well, now that you've got my number, call me up any time you want me.
Frank Thank you very much. I'll do that. Goodbye.
Teresa Goodbye.

Frank and Teresa put down the phones

Bob Who was that?
Fiona Who was that?
Teresa (*pleased*) No-one you know.
Frank Just a boy I was at school with, dear.

CURTAIN

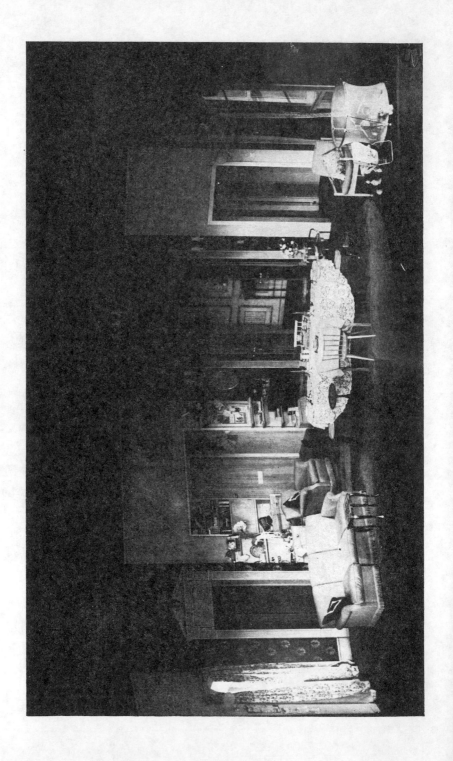

ACT I, SCENE 1

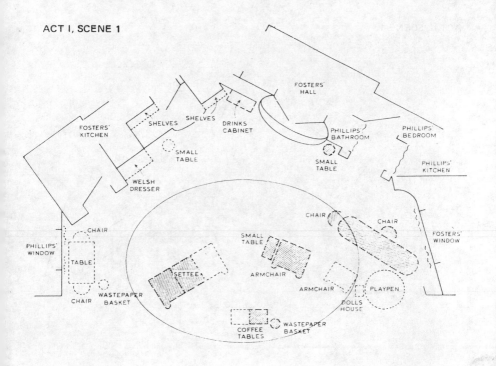

ACT I, SCENE 2

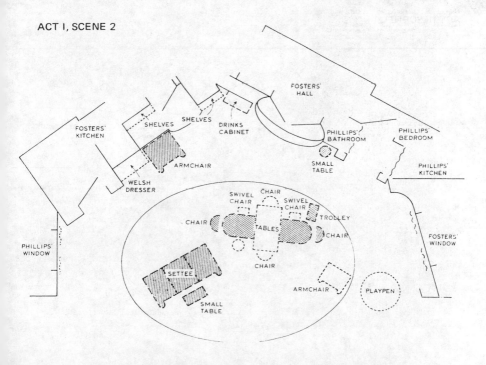

EALING GREEN CENTRE LIBRARY

ACT II, SCENE 1

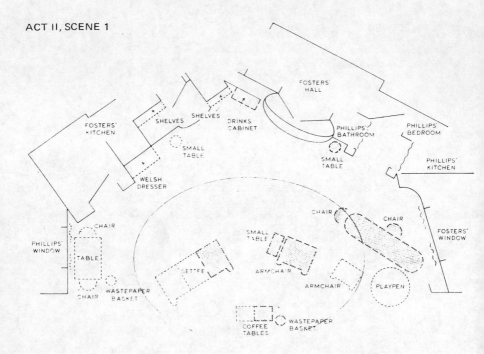

ACT II, SCENE 2

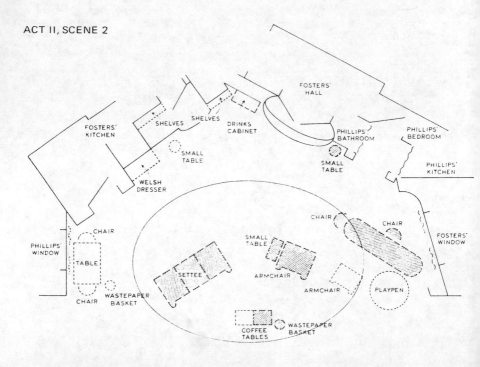

FURNITURE AND PROPERTY LIST

ACT I

Scene 1

On stage: Curtains at both windows closed to start

DR

Dining-table **(Phillips)**. *On it:* newspaper cuttings, letters, old news-papers, files, scissors, transistor radio, box of tissues. *Under it:* telephone directory

Two dining chairs. *On chair* DS *of dining-table:* **Bob**'s jacket with £5 note in pocket **(Phillips)**

Full wastepaper basket **(Phillips)**

DRC

Three-seater sofa. R two seats **(Foster)**. *On them:* cushions. L seat **(Phillips)**

UR

Shelves. *On them:* clutter of books, files, toys, etc. **(Phillips)**

Pegs with coats on them **(Phillips)**

Welsh dresser **(Phillips)**. *On it:* tin tray, cigarettes, matches, tumbler containing pencils, candle on plate, plates, similar clutter to that on shelves

Small table **(Phillips)**. *On it:* vase of flowers

UL

Drinks cabinet **(Foster)**. *On it:* silver tray containing full whisky decanter, two full sherry decanters, two whisky tumblers, six sherry glasses, bottle opener. *In it:* gin, Martini, orange juice, tonic water, ginger ale, soda water, spare bottle opener

Small table **(Foster)**. *On it:* vase of flowers

C

Armchair **(Foster)**

Small table **(Foster)**. *On it:* phone pad

DSC

Composite coffee-table. *On* L *section* **(Phillips)**: phone, ashtray, note-pad, pencil, dishcloth. *On* R *section* **(Foster)**: phone, notepad, pencil, kitchen timer, skipping rope, transistor radio, *TV Times*

Wastepaper basker **(Foster)**

L

Dining-table **(Foster)**

Two dining chairs **(Foster)**

DL

Armchair **(Phillips)**. *Over back:* apron

Child's playpen **(Phillips)**. *In it:* various toys

Baby walker **(Phillips)**
Baby chair **(Phillips)**
Doll's house **(Phillips)**. *In it:* **Bob**'s black shoe with toy squeaker in toe.

Off stage: In Kitchen R **(Foster)**
Tray. *On it:* two cups and saucers, two spoons, two small plates, two napkins, two knives, salt cellar, butter dish with butter, sugar bowl with sugar lumps, marmalade pot and spoon, silver coffee pot with coffee, silver milk jug with milk **(Fiona)**
Toast rack with toast, egg cup with boiled egg **(Fiona)**
Shoe-box **(Frank)**
Electric toothbrush, screwdriver **(Frank)**

UR
Outside front door **(Phillips)**
Copy of *The Guardian* **(Bob)**

UL
Outside double door **(Foster)**
Newspapers **(Fiona)**
Small gift-wrapped parcel containing perfume **(Frank)**
Frank's hat, coat and umbrella **(Fiona)**
Briefcase **(Fiona)**

L
In kitchen and bedroom **(Phillips)**
Mug of tea **(Teresa)**
Plate with sandwich **(Teresa)**
Copy of *The Guardian* **(Teresa)**
Large spoon **(Teresa)**
One black shoe **(Bob)**
One brown shoe **(Teresa)**
Blue file **(Bob)**
Boxes **(Teresa)**

Personal: **Fiona**: watch
Frank: watch

SCENE 2

Strike: Coffee-tables
Wastepaper baskets
Items from dining-table **(Phillips)**
Coffee mugs
Newspapers
Flowers from UR small table **(Phillips)**
Wrapping from perfume

Move: DR
Dining-table and two chairs **(Phillips)** to C
L
Dining-table and two chairs **(Foster)** to C
C
Chair **(Foster)** to UR

C
Small table **(Foster)** to DS of sofa

UR
Small table **(Phillips)** to DSR of dining-tables

Set: UC
Two swivel chairs

UL
Trolley **(Foster)**

UR
Pile of nappies

DR
All three seats of sofa **(Foster)**

C
On dining-table **(Foster)**: four place settings, cruet set, mat for serving
   dish, two candelabras with candles
On dining-table **(Phillips)**: four place settings including four soup
   dishes, mat for serving dish, salt and pepper, bottle of white wine,
   corkscrew

Off stage: Outside double doors UL **(Foster)**
Wet newspaper **(Frank)**

In kitchen R **(Foster)**
Tray with glasses and napkins **(Fiona)**
Frank's shoes **(Fiona)**
Four dishes of avocado **(Fiona)**
Opened bottle of wine **(Frank)**
Two vegetable dishes **(Fiona)**
Dish of frigadella **(Fiona)**
Four dinner plates **(Frank)**

Outside front door UR **(Phillips)**
Newspaper **(Bob)**
Carrier bag with tins of beer **(Bob)**

In kitchen and bedroom L **(Phillips)**
Tray with three tumblers and a packet of paper napkins **(Teresa)**
Mug of tea **(Teresa)**
Wet nappy **(Teresa)**
Tureen of soup with ladle **(Teresa)**

Personal: **William**: coat, hat
Mary: gloves, cardigan, coat

ACT II

SCENE 1

Strike: All dinner cutlery, etc.
Two swivel chairs
Trolley **(Foster)**

Re-set: All furniture as in Act I, Scene 1 except:
Sofa—two R seats **(Phillips)**, L seat **(Foster)**

Wash whisky and sherry glasses **(Foster)** and replace on drinks cabinet
Items on DR dining-table **(Phillips)**
Kitchen timer on DSC coffee-table **(Foster)**

Set: Sign on front door UR **(Phillips)** saying "Goodbye Forever"

Check: Curtains at both windows open to start

Off stage: Outside double doors UL **(Foster)**
Pram **(Frank)**
Dressbox. *In it:* dress with label **(Fiona)**
Monkey wrench **(William)**

In kitchen R **(Foster)**
Screwdriver, cup of coffee **(Frank)**
Cup of coffee **(Frank)**

In kitchen and bedroom L **(Phillips)**
Duster, dustpan and brush **(Mary)**
Mug of coffee **(Mary)**
Towel **(Bob)**
Vacuum cleaner **(Mary)**

Personal: **Frank:** watch
Teresa: handbag containing cigarettes and matches
Bob: belt in trousers

SCENE 2

Strike: Duster, dustpan and brush
Monkey wrench
Fiona's bag and gloves

Set: DRC sofa all three seats **(Foster)**

Re-set: Wash **William's** glass and replace on drinks cabinet

Check: Curtains at both windows open to start

Off stage: In kitchen R **(Foster)**
Two cups of coffee **(Fiona)**
Tray. *On it:* four cups, coffee pot with coffee, milk jug with milk,
sugar bowl with sugar lumps **(Fiona)**

In kitchen and bedroom L **(Phillips)**
Perfume **(Teresa)**

Personal: **Bob:** cigarettes and matches

LIGHTING PLOT

Practical fittings required: wall-brackets UL **(Foster)**, pendant **(Foster)**, wall-bracket L **(Phillips)**, pendant **(Phillips)**
Interior. Same scene throughout

ACT I, Scene 1   Early morning
To open: Dim light in living-room areas with bright early morning
effect from hall UL and kitchen areas

Cue 1	**Fiona** opens the curtains L	(Page 1)
	Bring up bright early morning effect L	
Cue 2	**Teresa** opens the curtains R	(Page 1)
	Bring up bright early morning effect R	

ACT II, Scene 2   Evening
To open: Evening effect from windows and outside front door UR
with interior light from hall UL and kitchen areas

Cue 3	**Teresa** switches on the light UR	(Page 24)
	Snap on pendant **(Phillips)** *and bring up interior lighting effect*	
Cue 4	**Fiona** switches on the light UL	(Page 24)
	Snap on pendant and wall brackets UL **(Foster)** *and increase interior lighting effect*	
Cue 5	**Teresa** switches on the light L	*(Page 27)*
	Snap on wall-bracket L **(Phillips)** *and increase interior lighting effect further*	

ACT II, Scene 1   Morning
To open: General effect of morning light
No cues

ACT II, Scene 2   Morning
To open: General effect of morning light
No cues

EFFECTS PLOT

ACT I

How The Other Half Loves 85

ACT II

Cue 18	**Frank** strides off to the kitchen R **Phillips'** *doorbell rings*	(Page 48)
Cue 19	**Frank** fishes for the timer in his coffee **Fosters'** doorbell rings	(Page 50)
Cue 20	**Mary** starts dusting **Phillips'** *phone rings*	(Page 55)
Cue 21	**Teresa:** "—that's all." **Phillips'** *phone rings*	(Page 59)
Cue 22	**Bob** and **Teresa** embrace **Fosters'** *doorbell rings*	(Page 60)
Cue 23	**Fiona:** ". . . out of this monstrosity." **Phillips'** *phone rings*	(Page 65)
Cue 24	**Fiona:** "Not a bite." **Fosters'** *doorbell rings*	(Page 68)
Cue 25	**Frank:** ". . . makes things a lot simpler." **Fosters'** *doorbell rings*	(Page 71)
Cue 26	**Teresa:** "My God!" *Long pause then* **Phillips'** *phone rings*	(Page 77)

MADE AND PRINTED IN GREAT BRITAIN BY
LATIMER TREND & COMPANY LTD PLYMOUTH
MADE IN ENGLAND